WILD FLOWERS
OF YORKSHIRE

Howard M. Beck

THE CROWOOD PRESS

First published in 2010 by
The Crowood Press Ltd
Ramsbury, Marlborough
Wiltshire SN8 2HR

www.crowood.com

British Library Cataloguing-in-Publication Data
A catalogue record for this book is available from the British Library.

ISBN 978 1 84797 164 7

Designed by Simon Loxley
Printed and bound in Singapore by Craft Print International

Contents

Introduction

Mention of Yorkshire evokes powerful sentiments. It is well known that Yorkshire is Britain's largest county – so large it has been politically divided into three areas. To the outsider traditionally it was a place of blunt folk, bleak wind-swept moors and dark satanic mills. But underlying this clichéd image is a very special place whose broad acres embrace widely diverse landforms. And the landscapes seen today, resulting from millions of years of geological upheaval, have been further modified by weathering and fine-tuned by millennia of industrial, social and agricultural land use.

Yorkshire embodies several distinct topographical zones. The landscape includes the Dales and moorlands in the west, the moors and rolling Wolds in the northeast, the industrial landscapes and former coal fields to the south, the cliffs and beaches of the North Sea coast. The county embraces two national parks, as well as many nationally important nature reserves, sites of special scientific interest, forest parks and other conservation areas.

Dramatic scenery aside, Yorkshire is home to some of the country's most stunning flowering plants, many of them nationally very rare. This diverse flora includes southern montane species, alpines and sub-arctic plants found nowhere else in England. Of the fifty or so British orchid species over half can be found in the region covered by this volume.

The idea behind this publication is to provide interested amateur botanists, ramblers and other curious country-goers with an easy to use, well laid-out guide detailing the habitats of Yorkshire and the plants most likely to be encountered. Additionally my wish is to provide a book that is simple to use, informative, and invaluable to anyone seeking to expand their knowledge base of the subject. Equally of course it is a book you can pore over in the comfort of your own home.

Perhaps more important, it is my sincerest desire to encourage a conservation-minded approach to the subject, and thus engender appreciation of wild flowers within their ecological context. For this reason I have followed the conservation ethos of not divulging the exact whereabouts of our rarest plants, for the enthusiast, with time and a developing knowledge of habitats, will eventually learn where to find these.

Many species now threatened were previously considered commonplace. It may be that with the advent of organic farming some of the old arable weeds will eventually make a comeback. This is already happening on a limited scale in parts of the North Yorkshire Moors and the Wolds, with species such as chicory returning from the brink of oblivion.

It is better to enjoy flowering plants in their natural surroundings where future generations can also share the pleasure. You should at all times resist any temptation to pick or uproot flowers. A flower picked before the seed has set will not reproduce. It is illegal to pick any wild flowers without a licence. Some species are so rare they enjoy special protected status, the violation of which is a criminal offence under British law. When examining hay meadows take care where you tread, if possible keeping to designated footpaths or the field perimeter.

Orchids in particular are especially sensitive to disturbance of their habitat. And it goes without saying that they should never be collected. Because of their unique fungal relationship most uprooted orchids simply die. Their obviously exotic nature was in the past the principal reason why some species received the attention of Victorian plant collectors. People uprooted specimens for their garden, and this dubious practice resulted in some previously widespread orchids becoming exceedingly rare. Indiscriminate collecting pushed the species of the lady's slipper to the verge of extinction.

Dandelions dominate the green in the Dales village of Arncliffe

When attempting to identify a plant always follow the maxim: take the book to the flower, not the flower to the book. Once you have identified it, you will probably want to photograph it for your records. Make a note of the species together with as many other useful details at the time, as identification from a photograph later can prove impossible.

Searching for wild flowers is one of the great unsung pleasures of the countryside, with little rivalling the buzz experienced when coming across a rare species for the very first time. Anyone can be an amateur botanist. It will not break the bank, nor do you need to be another David Bellamy to enjoy flowers. All you need is a keen eye, a 10x magnifier, notebook, a camera with macro facility, and this book.

HOW TO USE THIS BOOK

What format should a guidebook take? Fortunately, unlike animals, flowers stay still long enough for identification purposes, but a book organized into plant families may not be much help to the amateur lacking much field experience and knowledge of plant groupings. What about categorizing by colour or by flowering period? There are pitfalls with both these methods. For instance most flowering plants that are normally blue or purple will also produce flowers that are white, while red flowers have variations through pink to white, and white flowers may be pink-tinged. And some plants enjoy a very long season, flowering almost the whole year in some cases; in other instances the flowering period may vary due to, for example, micro-climates, latitude or altitude. Blooms may appear earlier or later depending on whether the season is early or late, the weather pattern wetter or drier than the norm. On balance, the format I prefer is the colour-coded layout, despite the fact some flower colours vary, so that is how I have organized this book.

There are over 400 species of flowering plants described here, with 300 full colour photographs. Within the description of each plant I have highlighted the main distinguishing features such as leaf structure; colour, number or arrangement of anthers, stigma and stamen, or indeed the petals and sepals; and also whether the plant is hermaphrodite (having both male and female reproductive organs). The flowering period is given as well as details about habitat and status. For ease of double-checking, similar species are given, which are often found nearby in the guide as they are in the same family.

Because orchids are rather special I have chosen to place these in their own section. Where a plant has several colour variants the photograph in each case shows the plant in its more usual livery. Where I have described distribution as commonplace, scarce, rare and such, this refers solely to the plant's frequency within the region covered by this book; for elsewhere in the country this may be the converse.

The plants are given a two-part name, in accordance with the Linnaean system of biological classification (devised by Swedish naturalist Carolus Linnaeus, 1707–78). The first part refers to the genus and the second the species. Both English and Latin names are provided along with the family to which it belongs, and any known colloquial names. The Latin names within square brackets indicate nomenclature used in the *New Flora of the British Isles*, by C. Stace, published in 1991.

I have included an index listing the plants by the most common English name and also the Latin equivalent. Appendices provide a glossary of botanical terms, additional reading matter and the names and addresses of useful organizations. Many of these bodies are actively engaged in conservation work, plant surveys and monitoring programmes. What finer way of repaying all the hours of enjoyment gained than by putting something back in return.

ABBREVIATIONS

sp:	species
ssp:	sub-species
agg:	aggregate , a plant belonging a larger group of closely related species or micro-species

NT:	National Trust
NYM:	North York Moors
NYMNP:	North York Moors National Park
PCNR:	Potteric Carr Nature Reserve
PDNP:	Peak District National Park
RNR:	Rodley Nature Reserve
SFNR:	Sprotborough Flash Nature Reserve
SP:	South Pennines
SPNNR:	Spurn Point National Nature Reserve
SSSI:	Site of Special Scientific Interest
VoM:	Vale of Mowbray
VoY:	Vale of York
YD:	Yorkshire Dales
YDNP:	Yorkshire Dales National Park
YWT:	Yorkshire Wildlife Trust

Botany is one of life's more pleasurable pastimes, and orchid hunting even more so. I hope the descriptions in this book will increase the enjoyment of anyone venturing into the countryside – whether for the first time or as a regular visitor – without the urge to remove plants for study away from the habitat.

WARNING

Many plants are poisonous. Neither the author nor the publisher recommends utilizing any part of a plant for culinary or medicinal purposes without expert guidance.

The Yorkshire setting

North York Moors

Some 70 per cent of the world's heather moorland surprisingly is located in England, and the UK's largest continuous expanse is found here in the NYM. It is a habitat with limited distribution both for Britain and Europe as a whole, and for this reason of great ecological importance.

Measuring approximately 32 km by 60 km, the NYM has an area of some 1,411 sq. km and corresponds more or less to that of the NYMNP, established in 1952 and the sixth to be so designated in Britain. The boundaries of the NYM can more or less be defined by a 41 km stretch of coastline forming the eastern cut-off, the Cleveland Plain to the northwest and the Hambleton Hills in the west and southwest, and by the Tabular Hills overlooking the Vale of Pickering to the south.

The area forms a relatively wild upland landscape, unique in character with its wind-scoured, flat-topped heather plateaux dissected by narrow valleys: Bilsdale, Newtondale, Farndale, Rydale being representative. With moorland being 34% of the total area (489 sq.km. of the land surface), this is the feature that has imparted to the region its identity.

Though most of the area exists above 210 metres a maximum height is reached at 454 metres on Urra Moor. From here elevation decreases to the east and along the southern fringe of the moors. Scarps, up to 298 metres high prop up the west and northern edge, with those at Sutton Bank and White Horse Bank being visible from as far away as Ilkley Moor.

Drainage tends to follow the principal valleys,

Many scarce plant species have been recorded from the disused Woodside Quarry, in Leeds, West Yorkshire

Ingleborough Hill, one of the Three Peaks, is a treasure
chest of rare species

those along the northern fringe, from Baysdale to Little Beck, draining into the Esk, and ultimately the North Sea at Whitby. South of the watershed, rainfall flows eventually into the Ouse via the Derwent, and other streams using valleys such as Bilsdale, Rosedale, Bransdale and Farndale.

The character of these moors, and the variety of wildlife supported, is governed to a great extent by the underlying geology. These rocks were deposited in warm seas some 195-140 million years ago. Rock types range from the limestones of the southern Tabular Hills, the sandstones of the moors, and the shales, iron stones and mudstones forming the northern scarps.

Almost a quarter of the area is swathed in natural woodland or planted conifer forest, mostly growing between the 119 and 238 metre contours, but established broad-leaf woods amount to as little as 7 per cent of the total. The Forge Valley west of Scarborough is an important habitat of this type. Arable land covers 318 sq.km while almost a quarter of the area consists of mostly unimproved grassland.

For the botanist the grasslands, broad-leaf woods, sheltered dales and hedgerows are most of interest. There are over 2,484 km. of hedgerows criss-crossing the area representing an important wildlife reserve. Areas with underlying limestone strata form the most prolific of habitat, so too the

The southwest edge of the Tabular Hills and North York Moors

disused quarries and abandoned railway trackbeds. Neither must one overlook roadside verges for these can also be a rich source of plants.

Almost half the flowers growing in Britain are also endemic to the NYM, however many more have disappeared over the decades due to intensive farming methods and habitat loss. Among the rarest species that may still be found, with perseverance, are pyramid, fly, bee and frog orchids, marsh helleborine, herb Paris, yellow archangel, viper's bugloss, baneberry and birdseye primrose.

The Wolds and East Coast

The Wolds extend inland from the sea cliffs at Bempton to form an arc curving around by way of Market Weighton to the Humber estuary at Hessle. They are predominantly rolling chalk hills of not more than 179 metres elevation. Like the NYM they are divided by steep-sided valleys, such as Thixendale and Burdale, but unlike the moors lack significant water courses.

The Wolds form some of the country's least spoilt landscapes, the soils being mostly free-draining by virtue of the underlying chalk. The area has few significant towns but many villages, and is

North York Moors and Farndale, famous for its swathes of wild daffodils

traversed by the 126 km. long Wolds Way footpath. Land use is predominantly arable, accounting for 1,023 square km. Woodland covers only 21 sq. km. and unimproved grassland some 27 sq km.

Being a calcareous landscape the Wolds share a similar calcicole[1] flora to that of the Yorkshire Dales. Most relevant are the grasslands, including verges, and also disused railway embankments and long-abandoned chalk quarries. Some hedgerows date back to the time of the Enclosure Acts (1750–1850) and are composed of hawthorn, dogwood and wild privet. Areas of scrub dot the area and have long been a feature of the landscape, comprising mainly hawthorn and gorse thickets.

Some of the more commonplace species a visitor may expect to find are kidney vetch, devils-bit scabious, salad burnet, agrimony, wood anemone, harebell, nettle-leaved bellflower, foxglove, purple toadflax and dog's mercury. Several species of orchids – frog, bee, pyramid, early purple – are endemic. One road side verge near Garrowby Hill is a riot of colour in mid-summer, with literally hundreds of orchids. The autumn gentian, bogbean and butterwort represent the scarcer inhabitants of the area.

With the exception of Spurn Point and the

[1] See the glossary for the definition of this and other botanical terms.

Humber littoral around Hull, the coastal strip is botanically less prolific. Coltsfoot, storksbill, common poppy, mallow, kidney vetch, pyramid orchid, northern marsh orchid and hairy tare are a few representative species of the cliff top plant communities, while sea rocket colonises the coastal driftline.

An important managed site of major interest to the plant hunter is the SPNNR (TA417151). It consists of areas of mature sand dunes, a lengthy sand and shingle spit, chalk grassland and mud flats. Although more famous for its bird populations there are plant communities of importance to the botanist. Yellow pimpernel, sea campion, sea rocket, and the cactus-like sea holly are endemic, so too the pyramid orchid. The environs of Hull city itself is also a rich source of plant life, including the not so common larkspur and lucerne.

The Vale of York

This transitional zone between the western Pennine Dales and the NYM and Wolds, forms a low-lying landscape with minor variations of elevation (up to 45 metres) created by surviving ridges of ancient glacial deposits marking the retreat points of the VoY ice sheet. Notable is the Escrick ridge about nine kilometres south of York.

Soils are complex and habitats varied: woodland,

Left: Limestone pavements, a repository of rare plants
Below: A colony of northern marsh orchids on chalk cliffs near Flamborough

Above: Patches of pink bistort in a Dales flower meadow
Right: A colourful flower meadow

Above: Bloody cranesbill occupying
a hollow in a limestone pavement
Left: The lush course of the river
Wharfe
Opposite page: Semerwater is one
of only three natural lakes

arable farmland, lakes, ponds, drainage dykes, flooded gravel pits, rivers, parkland and hedgerows. There is lowland heath too, though since the mid-eighteenth century almost 80 per cent of this habitat has disappeared. Destruction of water meadows (ings) too has been considerable, but some wet grasslands survive as a home for amphibious bistort, marsh ragwort, marsh marigold and other species.

Woodland mostly exists as plantation, with natural broadleaf woods confined to just a few isolated stands, mainly sycamore and birch. The VoY is foremost an arable landscape, divided by hedgerows that are predominantly haw and black-thorn, originating from the days of the Enclosures. Hedges formed from holly, hazel, dogwood and guelder rose are even older, with a few ancient but small, enclosed meadows dating from as early as the sixteenth century.

At first sight appearing sterile, there are nonetheless a great many species native to this area. Again roadside verges are a very important source

of plants. Species that can be expected include bluebell, cowslip, bitter vetch, pepper saxifrage, dog's mercury, common birdsfoot trefoil, creeping jenny, common sundew and ragged robin. Whole fields may occasionally be encountered ablaze with blooms of the common poppy.

One especially important habitat is the YWT's nature reserve at Askham Bog (SE575481), a site known for its relict fen and bog flora. It is situated just three kilometres southwest of York city. A mixture of scrubby woodland and wet grassland contribute much to the interest, with wetland being accessed by way of boardwalks. It is an abundant source of species including marsh pennywort, bog myrtle, water violet and common spotted orchid. There are also dramatic swathes of pink ragged robin and stately yellow flag.

Another area with a similar habitat and flora is that at Skipwith Common (SE668362), just off the A163 some 19 km. west of Market Weighton. For centuries this remnant glacial landscape was a

Top: Sweet cicely growing along a bridleway
Centre left: Wetland species colonising a disused limestone quarry
Centre right: Wild moorland heaths at the head of Nidderdale
Left: Archetypal landscapes of the Yorkshire Dales

Above: Broadleaf woodlands, a rich source of vascular plants
Right: Common spotted orchids dominate a roadside verge

source of fuel – wood and peat-cutting – for local communities. Today it consists of mixed broadleaf woods, fen, scrubby wetland, dry heath and a few small ponds. One of the more important plant inhabitants here is the small population of marsh gentian (*Gentiana pneumonanthe*).

West Yorkshire
With only 2,072 sq.km, West Yorkshire is smallest of the three political divisions forming the greater county. It includes the major conurbations of Leeds, Bradford and Wakefield, as well as many smaller satellite towns. The effects of the Industrial Revolution are everywhere to be seen in the canals and former textile mills. Some centres, like the Pennine village of Hebden Bridge, seem almost fortress-like in their hillside-hugging situation.

The underlying geology is predominantly Carboniferous in age, sandstones, mudstones and shales being dominant. Between Leeds and Tadcaster can be found a narrow corridor of magnesian limestone, the flora here reflecting this type of habitat. Throughout the county's southern-most reaches we find former coal pits and disused quarries. Some of the latter, for instance those at Micklefield, Crimsworth Dean and South Elmsall are now designated with SSSI status.

Moorlands are a dominant feature of the county.

Between these are the deeply incised valleys of Wharfedale, Airedale, Calderdale, Holme Valley (Summer Wine country), the Worth Valley and Crimsworth Dean, the latter craggy and heavily wooded. Rombalds Moor forms the important watershed between Airedale and Wharfedale and reaches a maximum elevation of 402 metres at Thimble Stones overlooking Ilkley.

The county is flanked by Lancashire to the west, by Greater Manchester in the southwest and by Derbyshire and South Yorkshire immediately to the south. There are several reservoirs, yet strangely for its size Yorkshire has only three natural bodies of water – Semerwater near Hawes, Malham Tarn and Hornsea Meer on the east coast.

Numerous nature reserves and protected areas have been established throughout the county: Fairburn Ings (SE451277), the RNR (SE227361) and Chevin Forest Park (SE203442) for example, but special mention must be made of Middleton

Woods close to Ilkley. It is the largest tract of ancient woodland in the county and unmatched for its early summer display of bluebells. The former sandstone quarry located at Woodside (NGR SE255383) is also important for the number of species supported.

South Yorkshire
With an area of 1,073 sq.km, South Yorkshire is predominantly a low-lying industrial landscape famous for steel production and former coal fields, major towns being Sheffield, Rotherham, Doncaster and Barnsley. In the far west of the county the higher moors of the South Pennines include a small slice of the PDNP, taking in Hallam Moors, Howden Moors and Langsett Moors. Highest elevation is reached on Outer Edge at 546 metres.

The geology resembles that of West Yorkshire. In the west the Pennine are covered with heather and blanket bog beneath which lie shales and sandstones. Moving further to the east towards

Opposite page: Cow parsley and rape growing alongside a hawthorn hedgerow
Above: Yellow iris and ragged robin growing in the wetland habitat of Askham Bog, the Vale of York

Above: The Potteric Carr nature reserve, South Yorkshire
Right: Typical rolling Wolds landscape

Above: Yorkshire moors: heather, bog asphodel,
tormental and sundew are typical plants of this habitat
Opposite page: Swathes of common poppy contrast
with a field of yellow rape

Lincolnshire, this strata is replaced by a sequence of sandstones, mudstones and shales belonging the coal bearing strata, while immediately east of Doncaster is the southerly continuation of the magnesian limestones found east of Leeds.

The principal river for the area is the Don, draining into the Ouse, its tributaries including the Dearne, Rivel, Loxley and the Rother. Disused coal mines and gravel pits dot the landscape along with patchy woodland, country parks and several conservation areas, some of them reclaimed industrial sites now forming important botanical retreats. Maltby Commons (SK550916), Dearne Valley SSSI (SE422022), Denaby Ings (SE498009) and Potteric Carr (SE599003) are among the better known.

Habitats variously include grasslands and flower meadow, marshlands, open water, woods, peat, bogland and fen. A large and diverse flora is endemic. Possibly the most significant of these conservation zones is that at Sprotborough Flash (SE537015). This is located beside the river Don near Mexborough, on a site resulting from mining subsidence. Since the mines closure it has developed into an especially prolific habitat, and visitors will have done extremely well to find most of the 500 species of flowering plants known from this reserve.

The Yorkshire Dales

When we talk of the Dales we immediately think of limestone, for it is this landform for which the region is best known. Over 300 million years ago the remains of myriad microscopic creatures were laid down in warm tropical seas. With time these accumulated marine deposits consolidated into the limestone that, after millennia of earth movements and weathering, give us the geographical features familiar today.

Established in 1954, and covering almost 1,813 sq. km., the Dales is internationally famed for its villages and scenery, not least, its spectacular dales and mountain landscapes. The latter include geological features such as Malham Cove, Trow Gill, Gordale Scar, dramatic waterfalls, deep caves and limestone pavements.

In essence a sheep farming community, the Dales have only 75 hectares of arable land and 94 km of hedgerows, of which a mere eight kilometres are species-rich. This is 0.2 per cent of the estimated national total. On the other hand the region is criss-

crossed by countless kilometres of dry-stone walls, one of the area's more recognisable features.

Dales countryside is varied and contrasting. By far the largest division is that occupied by improved grassland (445 sq.km.), closely followed by acidic grassland (472 sq.km.) and blanket and raised bog (352 sq.km.). One of the most significant habitats is scrub and broadleaf woods, which occupy 1,535 hectares. Mine spoil heaps cover 378 hectares while ponds and lakes just 45 hectares.

Besides the obvious limestone features there are important hay meadows and pastures (both upland and lowland), a few small wetlands, river valleys, peat moors and bogs, and the high gritstone-capped fells. Rocky limestone pastures in early summer form a mosaic of blooms with, for example, mountain pansy, early purple orchid, thyme, birdsfoot trefoil, milkwort and birdseye primrose. Limestone pavements too, are a crucial refuge for former woodland plants, baneberry, dark red helleborine and angular solomon's seal being indicative.

The dominant feature of the west is the Three Peaks, a group of hills better known for its annual walking event, and deep cave systems. That these same hills are a botanical treasure chest is a less well-known fact. The flora here will keep any self-respecting flower hunter busy for a lifetime. Some rarities include roseroot, marsh helleborine, sea campion, Pyrenean saxifrage and Yorkshire sandwort.

Progressing east from the Dales the limestone strata and moors give way to the gentler magnesian limestone landscapes, again a rich source of calcicole plants. The evocative ruins of Fountains Abbey and its grounds form particularly rich hunting for the enthusiast. On the walls several species have survived possibly from the days when Cistercian monks tended their own herbaceous borders.

Within the Dales area there are many very important reserves, some managed by the YWT, Natural England or the NT. The Ingleborough National Nature Reserve, Kilnsey Flush SSSI (SD974676) and Grass Wood (SD983652) in Wharfedale are three that spring to mind. There are many smaller sites: the tiny Globeflower Reserve (SD873667) for instance, is a real gem. A number of disused quarries are also being developed as reserves, though it will be many years before these become well established.

2
Flower hunting

Beside soil acidity there are many variables that regulate where a plant will or will not thrive. Familiarity with specific habitats will simplify searching for flowers. While some species thrive in very diverse conditions, others have more specialised requirements. For example the bluebell, though principally a woodland species, will be found growing beneath hedgerows or anywhere that woodland once was prevalent – open grassland in some cases. Bogbean prefers its feet in water, and therefore one would hardly search for specimens on disused railway embankments. Likewise, the acid loving heath plants of the Erica family will not tolerate base-rich soils.

Before a field trip always make a study of the habitat most likely to be favoured by the species being sought. Pre-armed with a modicum of such knowledge the plant hunter will quickly learn how to avoid wasting valuable time and energy tramping fruitlessly through inappropriate countryside.

Habitat
What exactly do we mean by habitat? Naturally we think of woodland, meadows, peat bogs and the like. But this is only half the picture. From a botanical standpoint we also have to take into consideration a whole gamut of variables that contribute to a viable environment. By this we mean latitude, altitude range, annual rainfall, exposure to prevailing wind, available sunlight, other vegetation cover and the pH value of the soil. The conditions under which plants will thrive are as different as chalk and cheese. Some prefer wet conditions, others thrive on unimproved grassland or broadleaf woodlands, still others are quick to colonise disused industrial sites, disturbed or waste ground.

One of the most important habitats is the flower meadow. Since the war traditional meadows throughout Britain have seen serious decline due to changing farming practises, including use of herbicides. Today only 5,000 hectares remain, and of these the most important are to be found in the Dales, notably in Wharfedale, Swaledale and Teesdale. Further east, there are one or two ancient, but small, meadows. In the predominantly arable Wolds, only 1.6% of the area is grassland with only a few scattered traditional meadows.

The plant types that may still be found in these meadows make an early summer visit a sheer joy. Contributing to the riot of colour are yellow rattle, self-heal, betony, meadow thistle, common birdsfoot trefoil, black knapweed, salad burnet and several species of orchid including fragrant, common spotted and greater butterfly.

Plants such as enchanter's nightshade, herb Paris and the secretive fly orchid are shade tolerant species, yet they still require some light for synthesis of food supplies. On the other hand scarce saprophytes derive all their nourishment from decaying plant debris of the forest floor, therefore are able to thrive in the deepest shade. They have no chlorophyll and are virtually pigmentless. Because of this, and the nature of their preferred home, these plants are extremely difficult to locate.

One of Yorkshire's richest flower habitats are old and well-established ash and hazel woodlands found throughout the region, and the rocky limestone pastures of the Dales. A similar diversity can be found on the magnesian limestones existing between the eastern Dales and the VoY, and in a narrowing band extending to the vicinity of Doncaster.

In the limestone pastures of the Dales endemic plants include numerous rare orchids, a few nationally very scarce. Some plants are only found in this area. Yorkshire sandwort (*Arenaria norvejica ssp.anglica*) for example prefers the short cropped limestone pastures of Ingleborough and has been confirmed nowhere else. The delicate birdseye primrose is found only in a narrow ecological zone

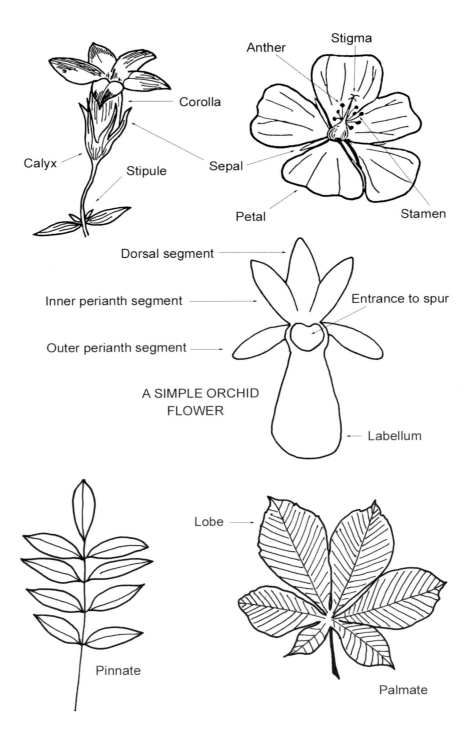

Corolla

Calyx

Stipule

Sepal

Anther

Stigma

Petal

Stamen

Dorsal segment

Inner perianth segment

Outer perianth segment

Entrance to spur

A SIMPLE ORCHID
FLOWER

Labellum

Lobe

Pinnate

Palmate

stretching across northern England, from Cumbria through the Dales and into the NYM.

Limestone pavements are a unique feature caused by glacier movements of the last Ice Age. The creeping ice mass scoured flat the limestone strata to leave pavement-like outcrops (clints) divided by numerous criss-crossing fissures (grikes). The finest and most extensive pavements are those to be found along the western fringe of the Dales, surrounding Ingleborough, at Moughton Scar, the head of Crummackdale, on Scales Moor, above the Cove in Malhamdale and towards Wharfedale.

Grikes may be up to three metres deep, and are an important refuge for many interesting plants formerly thriving in the ancient woodlands once covering the area. Baneberry, bloody cranesbill, herb robert and angular solomon's seal are typical. Grazing by sheep normally inhibits plant growth, but at Scar Close and Colt Park Nature Reserves, where sheep have been excluded for at least twenty years, the pavements have reverted to their former overgrown state.

Finally we must consider wasteland including old industrial sites such as disused mine tips. Wasteland in general often produces surprises, with new plants continually appearing. Cross 'contamination' of habitats can also occur when topsoil is transported to be used elsewhere, and domesticated plants become established in the strangest of places courtesy of gardeners who prefer to dump garden waste rather than composting.

Alien species that one might encounter include snowberry, garden daffodil, montbretia, shasta daisy, London pride, opium poppy, honesty, borage, Siberian iris and Pyrenean lily. Some species have become so well established that they now appear quite natural in the setting they have adopted.

IDENTIFYING FLOWERS

This book covers the majority of flowers most likely to be encountered, together with a selection of the scarcer plants added to whet the appetite of the amateur eager for more. Although this is a guide to plants and their habitats, I have purposely avoided divulging the whereabouts of our rarest species to discourage indiscriminate picking.

For equipment, all you need is a 10x magnifier, notebook, a camera with macro facility, and this book. A pair of binoculars may also prove useful in identifying plants that are inaccessible, on a cliff face for example.

The identification of flowering plants is one of the most satisfying aspects of being an amateur botanist. Sitting among the warm grasses with the buzz of insects and scent of flowers all about, with a brilliant sun burning in a cobalt sky, represents the essence of a balmy English summer day. Add to this the chance encounter with rare plants and you may find yourself hooked.

Identification of flowers demands some knowledge of plant structures. But do not be put off by this – it is not rocket science. Many factors should be considered, such as height, whether upright, prostrate, trailing, climbing or twining. The number, shape and arrangement of leaves, whether these or the stems are hairy, spiny, downy or otherwise, are a useful aid to placing a plant. The flowers themselves are not always the best clue to identity; umbellifers for instance, are all so similar that the beginner may experience difficulty separating individual species. The same applies to some orchids. Sometimes habitat is the only reliable indicator.

By Shape

As well as colour, flower shape is important. How many petals are there, and are they joined to form a corona? Is it composite, labiate or simple in structure? The various other organs of a flower must be closely examined too, for instance colour, shape and number of sepals; are the latter pointed, rounded or conjoined? Are bracts present? Are flowers solitary, upright, nodding, or in groups arranged in a loose inflorescence or tightly-packed spike?

In most cases flowers have both sepals and petals. The former are usually green and insignificant and the petals colourful and sometime spectacularly beautiful. Sepals are petal-like and normally form an outer whorl immediately beneath the petals. Where the sepals are joined to form a tube this is referred to as a calyx. Sepals can be almost hair-like, or in some instances coloured and larger than, or even replacing the petals, for example as with winter aconite, green hellebore and globeflower.

Flowers can have two or more petals, and where these are joined in a tube-like structure this is known as a corolla. Petals can be labiate – that is lipped as in the pea and mint family – pointed, rounded, notched or not, or strap-like as in the case with composites like the daisy and dandelion, when they are then called florets. In the case of composites the flower head is composed of a great many tiny flowers, the outer ones being known as ray florets, the inner ones, very many in number and forming a disk-like structure in appearance, are referred to as disk florets.

The male reproductive organs are called stamens, at the tip of which is the pollen-bearing anther. The colour of the latter can be an aid to identification. The female organs are the ovaries, each of which have one or more pollen receptive stigma, usually carried on a slender stalk-like style. The number and configuration of stigma and stamens should always be noted. Some flowers have both female and male reproductive organs, and are then referred to as hermaphrodite. In these the stamens form a ring around the stigma. In other cases stigma and stamens occur on separate flowers on the same plant, or on separate plants altogether.

By Leaves, Stems and Stipules
Plants may be spiny, downy, hairy, or hairless. *Leaves* can be lanceolate (spear-like), pinnate, palmate or palmate-lobed, heart-shaped, more or less round, with toothed or wavy margins – or not. *Stems* can be plain round, ribbed, square sectioned or winged. Take note of how leaves are arranged on the stem, whether they are alternate up the stem, in opposite pairs, clasping the stem or spirally arranged, in whorls or as a rosette at ground level. *Stipules* are small leaf-like organs located at the base of the leaf.

Some plants have root leaves that differ significantly from the stem leaves. Likewise plants that are both terrestrial and aquatic in nature often have two leaf forms. Some water plants have differing submerged and floating forms of leaf. In some cases plants have modified leaves, as in the insectivorous sundew and butterwort, where they are used to ensnare prey. Those of some species of legumes have leaves adapted to include extended tendrils at their tip to aid climbing.

ENDANGERED PLANTS

In Britain 345 groups of vascular plants – a staggering 20 per cent of the British total – have been classified as endangered by the UK's Joint Nature Conservation Committee. A report released by the JNCC in 2005 compared the 2002 survey New Atlas of the British and Irish Flora with a similar survey published in 1962. The comparison allowed scientists to measure the decline in plant populations across the UK over the previous forty years. The most worrying aspect of these results is that many species now threatened were previously considered commonplace.

PHOTOGRAPHING FLOWERS

Producing worthwhile images of wild plants requires a camera with close-up function. With old single-lens reflex (SLR) systems this involved fitting close-up attachments to an ordinary lens, or purchasing a macro-zoom. Many digital cameras have a macro facility that focuses down to within just a few centimetres. A point to bear in mind is that when in macro mode the depth of focus (sometimes referred to as the depth of field) is greatly reduced, therefore more care is needed when composing and focussing. A tripod is essential for a low-lighting situation; choose one that opens up right to ground level.

Try to take photographs that make a pleasing composition, if possible including some of the foliage. Avoid distracting backgrounds and do try to disturb the site as little as possible. If foliage or grasses have to be moved aside to take the photographs try to replace it as you found it.

It is worth noting that in strong sunlight petals will appear much brighter than the surrounding leaves. Therefore it will be necessary to compensate for this to avoid 'burning out' the flower and subsequently losing detail in the petals. This is especially so with yellow flowers. I find that I get better photographs of pale-petalled flowers under a bright overcast rather than in full sunlight.

A final bit of advice: Make a note of the species together with as many other useful details at the time, to avoid the frustration of trying to identify it later from the photograph. Always remember that it is illegal to pick any wild flowers without a licence, and when you are in the wild be careful never to trample wild flowers.

3

The flowers

▶ PURPLE SAXIFRAGE
Saxifraga oppositifolia
Family Saxifrage

Flowering period: March to April.
Distribution: Scarce: Only found in the
Three Peaks area of the Dales.

This is one of my favourite flowers, a pretty
addition to the early spring flora of the western
Dales. A native perennial alpine, this is one of
the most beautiful of the fifteen species of the
Saxifragaceae family endemic to our region. It
grows in damp places on limestone scars, crevices
and scree slopes between 400 and 600 metres
altitude, often providing a welcome splash of
colour pushing through late snow.
   It is fairly abundant on Penyghent and
Ingleborough, and also found in the screes and
scars of Moughton Fell. This mat-forming species
has trailing stems of 15 cm carrying opposite pairs
of small, tough, dark green oval leaves (5-10 mm)
typical of a plant used to roughing the elements.
The flowers are 10-20mm across with five petals
forming an almost unstalked, spreading bell.
Similar species: None.

▶ DUSKY CRANESBILL
Geranium phaeum
Family Geraniaceae

Flowering period: May to August.
Distribution: Occasional garden escape with
a scattering throughout in damp or shady
roadside situations.

This hairy, clump-forming perennial is sometimes
known as 'mourning widow'. It grows from 30 to
80cm in height with slender, branching stems
carrying light green palmate leaves (7-12 mm long)
with 5-7 roundly-toothed lobes. The base leaves
are long-stalked and occasionally brown-spotted,
the upper ones unstalked. Stipules are present.
The nodding flowers (2-3cm diameter) are
an unusual dark purple, indigo or blackish-maroon
with five oval pointed petals with wavy margins.
They grow in pairs in a terminal inflorescence.
There are five oblong to lanceolate green sepals,
a single stigma and a prominent column of ten
stamens with grey-blue anthers. Male and female
organs occur on separate flowers.
Similar species: None.

▶ WOOD CRANESBILL
Geranium sylvaticum
Family Geraniaceae

Flowering period: May to July.
Distribution: Common in the Dales, but becoming
increasingly infrequent further east. Very rare
in the NYM area. This plant is classified as a
nationally rare or threatened species.

This native perennial is one of the more attractive
of the dozen species of wild geranium native to
Yorkshire. It takes its name from the fact that
when the petals have fallen the remaining flowerhead, or fruit, resembles the head of a crane.
It was the source of study by Darwin, who
found that the plant can be either female or
hermaphrodite.
   Despite its name, this is a plant not solely
confined to damp woods, but also waysides and
unimproved grassland. Growing to heights of
70cm, it bears pretty flowers that are similar to
those of *G.Pratense*, but in this case purply-red
and smaller (15-25mm) often with a prominent
white centre. Both flowers and stalks are always
erect. Although palmately lobed the leaves differ
in being less deeply cut.
Similar species: See MEADOW CRANESBILL
(*G. Pratense*).

TOP: PURPLE SAXIFRAGE. BELOW LEFT: DUSKY CRANESBILL. BELOW RIGHT: WOOD CRANESBILL.

▶ COMMON DOG VIOLET
Viola riviniana
Family Violaceae

Flowering period: June to September.
Distribution: Found throughout the county, this is the most commonplace of the viola species. A delicate component of grassland communities: hedgerows, woodland and also open grassy places at altitude.

This attractive low perennial has almost hairless 2-10cm stems. Leaves, 5-80mm, are long-stalked forming a low tuft. They are heart-shaped with rounded teeth with normally toothed stipules. Growing in widely branching heads, the hermaphrodite flowers are 15-25mm across, pale purple or blue-violet, though white varieties exist.
　　Flowers have five spear-shaped sepals that are shorter than the five overlapping petals. The latter are usually streaked with darker purple, are unequal, the lowermost with a backward pointing 3-5mm long, stout, curving spur, often cream-coloured and notched at tip. The flower has five stamens and one stigma.
Similar species: EARLY DOG VIOLET (*V. reichenbachiana*) shares similar habitats, but is less common in the Dales (often mistaken for *V. riviniana*) and non-existent elsewhere. It has narrower leaves and paler, smaller (12-18mm) flowers. The latter have narrower petals and a purple spur that is not notched. Preferring a shady habitat.
　　TEESDALE VIOLET (*V. rupestris*) is a rare plant confined to a few calcareous localities on open ground on Ingleborough, and in Teesdale. It is a much smaller plant, with slightly downy, rounder leaves, and flowers (10-15mm across) having a pale violet spur.
　　HAIRY VIOLET (*V.hirta*) is fairly common from the Dales, but less so in the NYM and elsewhere. It has unscented blooms that are occasionally white. The plant has narrower leaves, no runners and longer stem hairs. Prefers scrubland and grassy places most often on lime.

▶ WILD PANSY
Viola tricolor
Family Violaceae

Flowering period: April to November.
Distribution: A scarce arable weed found only in Teesdale and a few other scattered locations on upland grasslands and rocky ledges. Mostly very rare or non-existent.

Also known as hearts-ease pansy, this beautiful little plant resembles a diminutive garden pansy. It is a variable short (up to 40cm) but erect biennial or annual being hairless or downy. The base leaves, 10-50mm, are long stalked, oval to almost spoon-shaped and scarcely toothed, while the stem leaves are short-stalked and narrowly oval or spear-shaped. Stems have pinnately lobed leaf-like stipules.
　　The bilaterally symmetrical flowers are 15-30mm diameter, hermaphrodite, and solitary from the leaf axil with two minute bracts. The five petals are longer than sepals and themselves are unequal, 8-19mm, the lowermost having a spur. Colour varies from a rich purple, violet, pink, white or yellow with purplish streaks. There are five stamens and one club-shaped stigma.
Similar species: See MOUNTAIN PANSY (*V.lutea*).

▶ SELF-HEAL
Prunella vulgaris
Family Labiatae

Flowering period: June to September.
Distribution: A very commonplace and widely distributed component of grassy places, bare ground, woodland clearings and road sides.

It was once believed to be a God-sent herb to drive out the devil and cure all manner of ailments. It is a low, creeping perennial herb with squarish stems growing to 30cm height and bearing leaves not unlike wild mint, that are 20-45mm in opposing pairs. They are pointed, roundish or oval and slightly toothed, the lower ones stalked. Hairs are short or absent.
　　The hermaphrodite flowers (10-15mm long) are purple, violet, or less commonly pink or white, growing in whorls of six forming oblong or square heads with purplish bracts at the base. The calyx consists of five sepals, the flowers have five petals to form a corona with two upper lobes joined as to be hood-like in appearance, the lower-most three bent backwards. There are four stamens and two stigma.
Similar species: Sometimes confused with BUGLE (*Ajuga reptans*).

TOP LEFT: COMMON DOG VIOLET. RIGHT: SELF-HEAL. BELOW: WILD PANSY.

❱ GROUND IVY
Glechoma hederacea
Family Labiatae

Flowering period: March until May.
Distribution: Common in lowland grasslands, hedgebanks and woods throughout the Dales and NYM but infrequent elsewhere. Recorded from Denaby Ings in South Yorkshire.

Also known as haymaids and catsfoot, this low, creeping native perennial is softly hairy, growing to 25cm. Stems have long-stalked heart- or kidney-shaped, blunt-toothed leaves in opposing pairs. The mat-forming, creeping stems are rooted at intervals, but angle upwards to flower. The latter appear in pairs or whorls of four at the leaf axils. Stipules are absent and bracts leaf-like.
　　The purple or bluish-violet hermaphrodite or female flowers are 15–22mm, with stalks shorter than the flower. There are five petals, 15–22mm, joined into a tube at the base, the upper two lobes almost hood-like. The lower three lobes are the larger. There are five almost equal sepal teeth, 5–6mm long, conjoined at the base. Flowers have two stigmas and five stamens beneath the upper lobes.
Similar species: SKULLCAP (*Scuttellaria galericulata*) is rarer, frequenting wet grassy places especially shady watersides. Infrequent in the Dales, more common towards the east, in the Washburn Valley, and also occuring in the Hull area and at Skipwith Common.

❱ CORN COCKLE
Agrostemma githago
Family Caryophyllaceae

Flowering period: June to August.
Distribution: Once a widespread arable weed, but rare now and only known from scattered sightings on the magnesian limestone. Unknown elsewhere.

This very attractive plant is tall (up to 1 metre) and covered in white hairs pressed close to the plant. The slender stems bear narrow, grass-like lanceolate leaves (45–145mm long) in opposing pairs. These are pointed, stalkless and have untoothed margins.
　　The trumpet-shaped blooms (up to 5cm diameter) occur solitary on long stems, and have five scarcely notched pale purple, mauve or magenta petals that have a paler base each marked with 2–3 broken darker veins. Five hairy sepals are joined in a calyx with long, slender teeth extending beyond the petals. There are six stamens.
Similar species: None.

❱ COLUMBINE
Aquilegia vulgaris
Family Ranunculaceae

Flowering period: May until July.
Distribution: Though less common in the NYM and other parts of the county, it enjoys a widespread distribution on cliff ledges, in woodlands and on scrub on calcareous soils in the Dales and on the magnesian limestones.

This magnificent but toxic plant is also known as granny's bonnet and granny's nightcap. It was the first of these species to be cultivated, sometime around the thirteenth century. Today there are pink and white domestic varieties, but in the wild they are always a rich purple-violet, any other shades definitely being garden escapes. It is a tall (up to 70cm) native perennial with trifoliate leaves, the leaflets being dull green and rounded. Each stem, which may be branched, has a group of two or more nodding flowers, dark purple in colour, all with inward and upward pointing nectar-bearing hooked spurs.
Similar species: None.

❱ LARKSPUR
Consolida ambigua
Family Ranunculaceae

Flowering period: June to September.
Distribution: A Mediterranean introduction once commonly cultivated in gardens, and which subsequently escaped to become naturalized. It is a rare and sporadic find from the Holderness and Humber area of the southern Wolds.

Growing to heights of 50cm, this perennial herb has downy stems carrying leaves that are finely divided into narrow segments, feathery-like, some of them arranged in whorls where the dark green stems branch. The very pretty hermaphrodite flowers are deep purple and arranged in a lax spike. There are five petals and a single long spur, the latter formed from one sepal and two petals. The flower stalks are equal in length to the bracts. All parts of the plant are very poisonous, with a few cases of horse poisoning occasionally reported.
Similar species: None.

TOP LEFT: CORN COCKLE. TOP RIGHT: COLUMBINE. BELOW LEFT: LARKSPUR. BELOW RIGHT: GROUND IVY.

❱ AUTUMN GENTIAN

Gentianella amarella ssp. amarella
Family Gentianaceae

Flowering period: July to autumn.
Distribution: Fairly evenly distributed through the southern parts of the NYM, the Wolds, the east coast, in the Craven area of the Dales and on the magnesian limestone.

Historically this plant has been used to treat digestive disorders. It was known in Roman times, when it was taken as medicinal tonic to heal galls, or 'felons', giving rise to the more common name felwort. This native biennial is the most common of our gentians and a fairly frequent find on unimproved short calcareous grasslands, well-drained chalk and occasionally on disused industrial sites.

The plant has branched stems and may grow to heights of 25cm but normally is much shorter. The flowers are dull purple and consist of upright bell-shaped blooms some 12–22mm long forming clusters from the base of the leaves. There are four to five petals with sepal teeth equal and pointed.
Similar species: FIELD GENTIAN (*G. campestris*) is rare. Similar in appearance but has blue flowers, and calyx has unequal sepal teeth, two of which are broader and overlap the remainder. Only in a few localities on the south side of Ingleborough.

❱ BITTERSWEET

Solanum dulcamara
Family Solanaceae

Flowering period: May to September.
Distribution: Very common along the magnesian limestone corridor and the VoY, notably Askham Bog. More scattered in the Dales and even less commonplace in the NYM and elsewhere. Found in woods and waysides, the banks of streams, scrub, hedgebanks and waste places.

Also known as woody nightshade, felon wood, dulcamara and erroneously as deadly nightshade, this clambering perennial relation to the tomato and potato reaches heights of two metres. It sports poisonous berries that are green first, then yellow before becoming vivid red when ripe, between September and October. These fruit were known in ancient times, examples having been discovered in the tombs of Egyptian Pharaohs.

The 10–15mm flowers are hermaphrodite and a rich purple with an obvious cluster of brilliant yellow anthers. The drooping flowers form loose clusters and have five pointed petals turning back at the extremity. Leaves are 30–100mm long, pointed oval, sometimes displaying two lobes at the base and arranged alternately on the downy stems.
Similar species: See BLACK NIGHTSHADE (*S. nigrum*).

❱ BUTTERWORT

Pinguicula vulgaris
Family Lentibulariaceae

Flowering period: Late spring to July.
Distribution: Very common on marshy ground, bogs, wet heath and flushes throughout the western Dales and as far east as upper Wharfedale. In the NYM and Wolds it is more scattered, and elsewhere virtually unknown.

The solitary purple or violet flower rises on a slender stem of up to 10cm from the centre of a starfish-like rosette of pale yellowy-green, fleshy leaves that are soapy to the touch. The flower consists of five unequal petals with a white streaked throat and a pointed spur.

This is one of six insectivorous plants endemic to Britain. The leaves, as many as twelve, are armed with glands that secrete a sticky fluid that ensnares small insects; enzyme-rich digestive juices released by additional glands then help digest the prey. Charles Darwin was the first to record that the leaf edges roll inwards towards the prey, but whether this plays a role in snaring insects in uncertain.
Similar species: None.

❱ LUCERNE

Medicago sativa
Family Leguminosae

Flowering period: June to October.
Distribution: Very rare throwback, and infrequent escape, from cultivation. It prefers waste ground or field margins usually close to habitation. Only a few instances of this species known in the county.

A member of the pea family, it is a medium (up to 90cm) height erect and practically hairless perennial formerly used as a fodder crop called alfalfa. It is a drought-tolerant species with slightly branching stems carrying alternate trifoliate leaves with slightly serrated, linear-oblong leaflets up to

TOP: BITTERSWEET. TOP RIGHT: AUTUMN GENTIAN. BELOW LEFT: LUCERNE. RIGHT: BUTTERWORT.

30mm long, broadest near the tip. Stipules are spear-shaped and toothed.

The hermaphrodite flowers (five to forty in number) occur in short racemes and range in colour through various shades of purple. They are 7–12mm long, slender with five petals (6–12mm), the lowest pair joined and side pair overlapping the lower ones. There are five equal sepals joined at base, with teeth equalling the calyx. There are ten stamens joined at the base and one club-shaped stigma.
Similar species: None.

▶ TUFTED VETCH
Vicia cracca
Family Leguminosae

Flowering period: June to August.
Distribution: Widespread on rough grassland, roadsides, in hedgebanks and scrub throughout the NYM, the Dales and on the magnesian limestone corridors. More scattered in the Wolds and South Yorkshire.

A clambering (to 120cm) native perennial with straggling stems having slightly downy, opposite leaflets (5–30mm long) in eight to twelve pairs, like a ladder terminating in tenacious branched tendrils, that aids climbing.

Flowers are hermaphrodite, 10–12mm long and pea-like. These are purple or blue-violet, grouped ten to forty in a single-sided spike. There are five sepals 2–6mm long forming a calyx. Five petals consist of a joined lower pair, the side petals overlapping, the uppermost one being the largest. There are ten joined stamens and one stigma.
Similar species: BUSH VETCH (*V. sepium*) is similarly common, shares a similar habitat, has ladder-like leaves with terminal tendrils, but the flowers form smaller blue-purple spikes, very rarely yellow. Leaflets form three to nine pairs, the flowers number two to six in a shorter spike. Flowers from April to November.

▶ DEVILSBIT SCABIOUS
Succisa pratensis
Family Dipsacaceae

Flowering period: June to October.
Distribution: Very widely distributed in the NYM and the western Dales, but tailing off into the magnesian limestones between there and the VoY. Also known from north-facing slopes in the Wolds, the east coast and parts of South Yorkshire.

A frequent plant of unimproved grassland, damp woodland fringes, forest rides and roadsides. This native hairy perennial grows to 80cm with slightly branching stems. The latter have elliptical untoothed leaves that are stalked and sometimes blotched bluish-purple. The upper leaves are generally narrower and occasionally slightly toothed, the lower ones forming a rosette.

The pincushion-like flowers are 15–25mm in diameter, solitary and coloured purple, bluish-purple or lilac, rarely pink in rounded heads that appear neater than other scabious species. Tradition has it that the name is derived from the fact that the devil bit off the roots of the plant in his anger at the Virgin Mary. According to seventeenth century herbalist Nicholas Culpeper the root, if boiled with wine, was an especially powerful protection against plague.
Similar species: SMALL SCABIOUS (*Scabiosa columbaria*) is very common in the Craven area of the Dales, but less so in the NYM and other areas. It has paler flowers and pinnately lobed leaves.

▶ MUSK THISTLE
Carduus nutans
Family Compositae

Flowering period: June to September.
Distribution: Scarce. A plant with scattered distributed in the southern and southwestern parts of the NYM, the Hambleton Hills, the Wolds and on the magnesian limestones east of the Dales.

This is a hermaphrodite plant, also known as nodding thistle, of free-draining calcareous grassland, roadsides and along woodland fringes. A handsome, tall biennial popular with finches, with winged stems (growing to 1 metre) that are spiny and cottony, while the long-spined leaves are deeply pinnately lobed. The flowerheads are bright purple, 35–50mm across, usually growing solitary and drooping (hence the alternative name) and fringed with purple-tinged, spiny bracts.
Similar species: None.

▶ GREATER KNAPWEED
Centaurea scabiosa
Family Compositae

Flowering period: June to October.
Distribution: Common along waysides, hedgerows, in unimproved grassland, meadows and in disused quarries on base-rich soils. Found

TOP LEFT: MUSK THISTLE. TOP RIGHT: DEVILSBIT SCABIOUS. MIDDLE LEFT: TUFTED VETCH. BELOW AND INSET: GREATER KNAPWEED.

in the magnesian limestones east of the Dales and along the southern fringe of the NYM. There is also a scattering in the Dales, the VoY, and also from the Rodley Nature Reserve in Leeds.

This hardy, medium-height perennial has wiry and furrowed stems (30–90cm high) carrying sparsely bristled leaves that are pinnately lobed, the latter enlarged upwards. The lowermost leaves are long-stalked and form a clump at the base of the plant; the upper ones unstalked.

The thistle-like flowerheads, apparently rayed, are shaggy-looking and solitary, being purple in colour and 30–50mm in diameter. The scale-like bracts are green with black hairs on the margin.
Similar species: See PERENNIAL CORNFLOWER (*C. montana*).

❱ BLACK KNAPWEED
Centaurea nigra
Family Compositae

Flowering period: June to September.
Distribution: A relation of the common daisy, this abundant component of tall dry grassy communities is found throughout the county in sunny positions beside roads, in hedgerows, railway cuttings and waste places.

Also known as lesser knapweed, common knapweed or hardheads, this native perennial reaches heights of 70cm and resembles a thistle but lacking the spines, instead having robust hairy stems. These bear spirally arranged lanceolate leaves, the lowermost finely toothed. It has rayless, brush-like flowerheads of 15–20mm, purple or purplish-pink, appearing solitary or in clusters, a source of nectar for bumblebees and various species of butterflies. The plant has blackish or dark brown sepal-like bracts with long slender teeth. Formerly used as a balm for bruises and scrapes.
Similar species: SAW-WORT (*Serratula tinctoria*) is not as common, having an infrequent distribution in the Dales and Wolds. Elsewhere it is at risk of disappearing altogether. It is a more slender plant growing 30–90cm tall, with pinnately lobed leaves finely toothed, hence the name. Flowers always grow in clusters and are a paler purple with sepal-like, purplish-tipped bracts and scales between the florets. Male and female flowers occur on separate plants. Flowers from July to October in woodland margins, damp grassland and marshes on calcareous soils.

❱ LESSER BURDOCK
Arctium minus agg.
Family Compositae

Flowering period: July to September.
Distribution: Widespread in waste places, grassland, open woods, scrub and roadsides throughout the VoY, on the magnesian limestones, the NYM and in the Dales below 300 metres, though less common in the latter.

This medium-tall, downy branching biennial has robust arching, spineless stems carrying broadly heart-shaped leaves some 30–400mm in length, arranged spirally. Lower leaves have long, hollow stems, the upper ones short-stalked. The purple, thistle-like flowerheads, 15–30mm, are rayless, egg-shaped and occurring in short-stalked spikes.

Tiny, hermaphrodite florets enclosed by sepal-like hooked bracts form burs after the flower has died back. Sepals are hair-like; five petals form a corona with five stamens and one stigma. Leaves boiled and cooled were used to make a drink.
Similar species: GREATER BURDOCK (*A. lappa*) is more common on marginal ground in the VoY, but rare in the Dales. It has much larger (35–40mm) globular flowers and blunter leaves that are as long as they are broad.

❱ PURPLE TOADFLAX
Linaria purpurea
Family Scrophulariaceae

Flowering period: June to August.
Distribution: An attractive species originally introduced from the Mediterranean as a garden plant. Since then it has become well-established but scattered in the NYM, VoY, the Wolds and less commonly in the Dales.

A hairless perennial of waste places, railway embankments, gravely places, wall footings, roadsides and stony banks mostly close to habitation. The greyish stems, growing to heights of 80cm, bear linear untoothed, grey-green leaves that are alternate and numerous. The blooms are 8–10mm long, deep purple, or violet (rarely pink) with five petals and a long slender, curving spur. They grow in tall spikes of twenty to thirty flowers that are particularly attractive to hoverflies, bees and some species of daylight flying moths.
Similar species: None.

TOP AND INSET: LESSER BURDOCK. BELOW LEFT: BLACK KNAPWEED. BELOW RIGHT: PURPLE TOADFLAX.

❯ SMALL SCABIOUS
Scabiosa columbaria
Family Dipsacaceae

Flowering period: June to October.
Distribution: Common to the Dales but less so east of there, on the magnesian limestones, the NYM and elsewhere in the county.

This very attractive plant frequents well-drained limestone grasslands, ledges on cliffs and disused quarries. Also called a pin-cushion flower, it is a variable native perennial that grows to heights of 65cm. The rarely branching, hairy stems rise from a rosette of pinnate leaves that are narrowly lobed, with stem leaves divided into narrow lobes.

The flowers are solitary with a rather flattish lilac head 15–25mm across, having five petals to each floret. There are dark bristles among the florets and a single row of bracts. Herbal cures reduced from the plant were said to be good for scabies and to keep the heart free from any infection of pestilence!
Similar species: FIELD SCABIOUS (*Knautia arvensis*) is more commonplace in the Dales and NYM, and scattered elsewhere. It is taller (80cm), more branched and has larger (30–40mm) flowers with only four petals per floret. Leaves are up to 30cm long, hairier than *S. columbaria* and divided into pairs. The flowers are hermaphrodite, with the outer florets much more prominent than in *S. columbaria*. Has similar flowering period but prefers roadsides, hedgerows as well as waste places.

❯ TEASEL
Dipsacus fullonum
Family Dipsacaceae

Flowering period: July to August.
Distribution: Not that common in the Dales, but increasingly so further east into the magnesian limestone belt and beyond, in the VoY. In the NYM, the Wolds and coastal fringe the species only rarely occurs.

An impressively tall hairless biennial growing to heights of 3 metres on robust prickly stems. Its normal habitat is damp grassy places, bare and waste ground, but also includes road cuttings. Leaves are 400mm lanceolate and covered with whitish pimples, and form a basal rosette with narrower leaves paired up the stem, often clasping at the base and sometimes toothed.

Flowers (10–15mm long) are hermaphrodite, pale purple and grow in an ovoid matrix forming a spiny head 25–75mm long. Four mauve petals form a tube, with two to four stamens and one stigma. The tiny sepals form a cup-like rim. Several prominently pointed bracts curve upwards around the flower head from the base. A sub-species of the teasel was once cultivated for the wool carding process of the textile industry.
Similar species: SMALL TEASEL (*D. pilosus*) is rare. Found in only a couple of locations in Dales deciduous woodland. A medium-tall biennial with oblong stalked leaves and round flowerheads that are white, woolly and spiny with violet anthers.

❯ COMMON COMFREY
Symphytum officinale
Family Boraginaceae

Flowering period: May to June.
Distribution: Abundant along roadsides, in grassy places, ditches and beside water throughout the area, but scattered and nowhere common.

Also known as great comfrey, this tall plant (up to 2 metres) is well-branched and a softly hairy, stout perennial with broad lanceolate leaves of 40–250mm, carried alternately on winged stems. The root leaves are the longest, and stemmed. The plant feels rough to the touch, like sandpaper. Flowers are 15–20mm, hermaphrodite, usually mauve, lilac or less commonly white, in bell-like, drooping, forked clusters. Flowers have five pointed sepals forming a calyx, five equal petals joined in a corona with five stamens and one stigma.

Nicholas Culpeper spoke of the plant's herbal benefit to those with 'inward' hurts, bruises, ulcers of the lungs and other wounds, and advised that partaking of a decoction of the root, boiled with wine or water, would ease the patient's suffering.
Similar species: TUBEROUS COMFREY (*S. tuberosum*) is rare, much smaller and often with unbranched stems. The flowers are yellowish-white, never mauve or pale purple, with pointed sepal teeth three times longer than the corolla. Usual habitat is damp, shady ground.
RUSSIAN COMFREY (*S. uplandicum*) is a widespread escape from cultivation, a hybrid between *S. officinale* and *S. asperum* that was introduced into Britain as animal feed about 1870. Fairly common in the NYM and VoY, but rare

TOP LEFT: SMALL SCABIOUS. TOP RIGHT: TEASEL. BELOW: COMMON COMFREY.

anywhere else. It has stiffly hairy winged stems, the wings being narrower than in *S. officinale* and not extending as far as the next leaf node. Flowers are blue or purplish-blue.

▶ LUNGWORT
Pulmonaria officinalis
Family Boraginaceae

Flowering period: March to May.
Distribution: Scarce. A garden escape that is established in a few locations throughout the county, mostly in shady places beside roads and in open woodland.

This pretty plant grows to heights of 30cm and is also known as the Jerusalem cowslip. It is a short, downy plant producing horizontal creeping rootstock with bristly stems carrying alternate, oval leaves that are dark green in colour. The leaves, narrowing at the base, grow mostly from the base of the plant, and are larger than stem leaves, which are stemless and clasping.

The bell or funnel-shaped flowers – lilac, sometimes turning steel blue – are very similar to common comfrey, and grow in terminal clusters. But where the plant differs from comfrey is in the leaves, which are lanceolote or heart-shaped and covered with white or pale pink spots and blotches. As the name suggests, this species was once thought medically beneficial for respiratory complaints.
Similar species: None.

▶ IVY-LEAVED TOADFLAX
Cymbalaria muralis
Family Scrophulariaceae

Flowering period: May to September.
Distribution: This plant was first recorded as a rock garden plant in Britain in 1640 but is now widely established in the wild, growing in patches on bridge parapets and walls.

It is one of the smallest but most attractive members of the figworts, being a trailing or drooping, hairless perennial. Stems grow up to 80cm in length and have palmately lobed leaves that are ivy-like in shape and long-stalked. They grow on alternate sides of the stem, the lowermost being paired.

The delicate two-lipped blooms are 8–10mm long, almost orchid-like in appearance, lilac-coloured with a yellow spot, and have a short spur that is tipped with dark purple. They grow singly from a leaf axil and have no bracts. The flower stalk is significantly longer than the flower. The latter has five 2–2.5mm-long sepals and five 9–15mm-long petals, four stamens and one stigma.
Similar species: None.

▶ PALE TOADFLAX
Linaria repens
Family Scrophulariaceae

Flowering period: June to September.
Distribution: Scattered. A plant recorded from waste ground, walls and dry, sparsely grassy places. Not very common in the Dales, West Yorkshire and the Wolds, but absent from the NYM and elsewhere.

It is a native perennial of calcareous soils growing to 60cm. The often branching, greyish stems have linear leaves that are untoothed and numerous up the stem, usually alternate. Flowers are pale lilac with darker purple streaks, or veins, with an orange spot on lower lip. The spur is short and curved, some 7–14mm in length. Flowers occur in loose spikes at the tip of the main stem, and also from lower leaf axils.
Similar species: None.

▶ HEATH SPEEDWELL
Veronica officinalis
Family Scrophulariaceae

Flowering period: May into mid-summer.
Distribution: Common. This, the smallest and least conspicuous of the speedwells, is found in dry grassland, open woods and heaths throughout the area covered by this book.

This low (up to 10cm), mat-forming, creeping perennial differs from other speedwells in having its flowers growing in an upright, but crowded, spike emerging from the prostrate stems, the latter readily rooting at nodes. Leaves are short-stalked, oval or elliptical and slightly-toothed, with both stalks and leaves softly covered in fine hairs.

The blooms (8mm across) are a delicate shade of lilac shot through with darker veins or purple. They are comprised of four equal sepal lobes and four unequal petals. The flowers are a valuable source of nectar and pollen, attracting bees, hoverflies and flies.

TOP LEFT: PALE TOADFLAX. TOP RIGHT: LUNGWORT. BELOW LEFT: HEATH SPEEDWELL. BELOW RIGHT: IVY-LEAVED TOADFLAX.

Similar species: See THYME-LEAVED
SPEEDWELL (*V. serpyllifolia*).

▶ WATER VIOLET
Hottonia palustris
Family Primulaceae

Flowering period: May to July.
Distribution: Absent from the NYM and
elsewhere confined to shallow pools, ponds and
similar wetland habitats. Recorded from mid-
Wharfedale and from Askham Bog in the VoY.

This is an attractive aquatic perennial growing to
heights of up to 90cm. The stems are floating or
submerged with leaves (20–130mm) that are
pinnate and cut one–two times into slender,
feathery lobes. They are arranged around the stem
and are practically hairless and absent of stipules.
The stems turn upright out of the water to flower.
    The Hermaphrodite blooms (three to eight in
number) are arranged in a lax spike and are lilac,
mauve, pale pink or violet with a yellow centre.
They are 20–25mm in diameter with five, slightly-
notched petals (12–17mm long) joined at the base.
There are five narrow sepals (5–10mm long), five
stamens and one, club-shaped stigma.
Similar species: None.

▶ DAME'S VIOLET
Hesperis matronalis
Family Cruciferae

Flowering period: May to August.
Distribution: A naturalized garden escape
introduced to Britain from southern Europe.
Today it has a fairly broad distribution throughout
the county on riverbanks, woodland fringes,
hedgebanks, roadsides or waste ground, especially
near habitation.

Sometimes known as sweet rocket, this medium to
tall (up to 80cm) hairy perennial or biennial
prefers moist locations with a hint of shade. The
short-stalked lanceolate, dark green leaves are
toothed and arranged alternately on the stems.
The flowers occur in loose clusters and can be
lilac, mauve or white, being 15–20mm across with
four equal petals. In the evening the strongly
fragrant blooms give off a scent especially
attractive to moths. During daytime they attract
cabbage white and orange-tip butterflies.
Similar species: Easily confused with HONESTY

(*Lunaria annua*) which is taller (up to 1.5 metres)
with larger, 25–30mm, purple or dark pink flowers
appearing from April into May.

▶ VERVAIN
Verbena officinalis
Family Verbenaceae

Flowering period: July to September.
Distribution: Extremely rare. This herb is an
introduction in the north and only known from a
couple of locations in the Dales and West
Yorkshire. Usual habitat is roadsides and dryish
waste places.

Also known as Juno's tears, pigeonweed and
enchanter's plant. It is a short to medium height
(50cm) roughly hairy, slender perennial bearing
deeply pinnately lobed leaves that are unstalked,
toothed and grow in opposite pairs on square
stems. The tiny two-lipped flowers are lilac or
lilac-pink coloured, with five-lobed petals in long
slender spikes, often growing from the leaf angles.
    Vervain has long been held to have special
properties and was one of the herbs sacred to
Celtic druids. It was once thought a female
aphrodisiac. The plant had many herbal
applications, not least the treating of snake bites,
or as an infusion for the bathing and soothing of
skin infections. It was also attributed magical
properties as a folk charm against evil.
Similar species: None.

▶ WILD BASIL
Clinopodium vulgare
Family Labiatae

Flowering period: June to September.
Distribution: Fairly widespread throughout the
county on unimproved calcareous grasslands.

A pleasant smelling wild herb (not the basil of
culinary popularity) common to the mint group of
plants. It is a bushy and upright native perennial
often found alongside marjoram in lightly shaded
limestone and chalk habitats – woodland fringes,
hedgerow bottoms, scrubland and grassy plant
communities. The name comes from the Greek
basilikon, meaning 'kingly'.
    Growing to heights of 60cm, this softly hairy
plant is scarcely branched with leaves that are
pointed oval, stalked and slightly toothed. Flowers
are mauve or lilac, growing in dense whorls at the

TOP: WATER VIOLET. BELOW LEFT: DAME'S VIOLET. CENTRE: VERVAIN. RIGHT: WILD BASIL.

base of the upper leaves. There are bristle-like bracts and a purplish sepal tube covered in white hairs.
Similar species: See MARJORAM (*Origanum vulgare*).

MARJORAM
Origanum vulgare
Family Labiatae

Flowering period: July to September.
Distribution: Widespread throughout the county on unimproved calcareous grasslands and on chalk strata. Slightly more common than wild basil.

Also known as oregano, this is an agreeably aromatic plant. It is a native perennial of medium (up to 60cm) height usually found along roadsides, dry woodland fringes, in scrub and on rough grassland and disused limestone quarries. The leaves are stalked and oval with slight teeth. Flowers are mauve or lilac with dark purplish bracts and grow in loose, branched clusters.

Though this can be used as a culinary herb, it is not so sweetly tasting as the cultivated varieties. An infusion of the leaves together with those of thyme, lavender, hyssop and honey apparently soothes hay fever. A sprig or two hung in a doorway will repel insects.
Similar species: See WILD BASIL (*Clinopodium vulgare*).

WILD THYME
Thymus polytrichus
Family Labiatae

Flowering period: May to August.
Distribution: Very commonplace in the Dales and along the southern fringes of the NYM. Scattered in the Wolds and elsewhere.

A culinary herb of short cropped turf and rocky ledges, usually on calcareous soils, where it forms a prostrate, mat-forming undershrub. The straggly stems may be up to 7cm in length with short-stalked oval leaves, often quite woolly in appearance. Flowers are lilac or purplish-pink forming aromatic round heads. Tea made from this plant at night-time is reputed to prevent nightmares. An infusion of the leaves is also reputed to relieve headaches.
Similar species: None.

CREEPING THISTLE
Cirsium arvense
Family Compositae

Flowering period: June until September, or later.
Distribution: Extremely common in the Dales, Three Peaks area, along the magnesian corridor east of the Dales and into the VoY and Wolds. It is also known from West Yorkshire but absent in the NYM.

An abundant native perennial of tall grassland communities, waste ground, roadsides and, much to the annoyance of hill farmers, as a persistent weed of pastures everywhere. Normally hairless and unbranched, this relative of the daisy can grow to heights of one metre. The male and female flowers usually appear on separate plants.

The stems are spineless and scarcely branched, the leaves deeply pinnately divided, spiny and often cottony on their under surfaces. Flowers (15–25mm) are lilac and rayless, forming brush-like heads in clusters. Beneath the florets the scale-like browny-purple bracts are scarcely spiny.
Similar species: SAW-WORT (*Serratula tinctoria*) is much rarer with a scattering of locations in Craven and even less so, in the North York Moors and Wolds areas. It is a more slender, hairless plant growing 30–90cm tall. The flowers are a paler purple with sepal-like purplish-tipped bracts and scales between the florets. Male and female flowers are on separate plants. Leaves are pinnately lobed with lobes finely toothed, hence the name. Flowers from July to October along woodland margins, damp grassland and marshes on calcareous soils.

SPEAR THISTLE
Cirsium vulgare
Family Compositae

Flowering period: July to September.
Distribution: Extremely common throughout the county on unimproved grasslands, waste ground and as a weed of roadsides and cultivated ground. Absent from the high moors.

This plant can grow to almost 1.5 metres, and as a biennial is about as spiny as they come, carrying 150–300mm deeply pinnately lobed, spear-like leaves arranged spirally around winged stems. Leaves are cottony in appearance underneath. Flowers are hermaphrodite, up to 40mm across,

TOP LEFT: SPEAR THISTLE. TOP RIGHT: WILD THYME. BELOW LEFT: CREEPING THISTLE. BELOW RIGHT: MARJORAM.

with florets forming brush-like lilac or reddish-purple heads, often growing solitary. The bracts are usually hairless and yellow-tipped.
Similar species: None.

▶ GIANT BELLFLOWER
Campanula latifolia
Family Campanulaceae

Flowering period: July to September.
Distribution: A plant of limestone hills and mountains, mainly in older woodlands, riverbanks and damp hedgerows in partial shade. Very common in the Dales and on the magnesian limestones to the east. Also fairly abundant in the NYM, but concentrated more to the northeast and in the Hambleton Hills.

And what a handsome plant this native perennial is, with its spike of lilac-blue bells. Growing to a height of one metre, the stout, slightly furry, angled stems bear spear-shaped, evenly toothed short-stemmed leaves. The lowermost leaves are rounded or tapered at the base.

The flowers are particularly fine and appear solitary at the base of the upper leaves, the lowest blooms opening first. The five pointed petals join into a flaring bell-shaped corona 40–50mm long that makes a wonderful display. The flowers are lilac or violet-blue, occasionally white.
Similar species: NETTLE-LEAVED BELLFLOWER (*C.trachelium*) is rare and shares a similar flowering period and habitat, but known from only a few locations. It has similar angled and hairy stems, carrying much broader, irregularly-toothed lanceolate leaves. Flowers are smaller (30–40mm long), formed one to three in a leafy spike, appearing from July into September in woods, hedgebanks and scrub.

▶ HAIRY TARE
Vicia hirsuta
Family Leguminosae

Flowering period: May to August.
Distribution: Scattered in the Dales and NYM on open grassland, waste ground or arable fringes as well as clifftop grass communities along the coast. It can be found on rail track ballast along the Esk Valley and from the southern extremities of the Wolds.

A frequent but very fragile, almost hairless annual. The short (up to 30cm, rarely 70cm) stems have an end tendril, mostly branching, to aid twining among longer grasses. Leaves are pinnate with four to ten pairs of alternate leaflets, each with a tip that is squarish or notched. Leaf stalk is virtually absent.

The small (2–5mm) pale lilac or dull white flowers are hermaphrodite, usually formed one to eight in a spike originating from a leaf axil. Bracts are absent, but flowers have five sepal teeth that are longer than the calyx tube. There are five petals 4–5mm long, the lowermost two joined, and two side petal overlapping at base. Flowers have one stigma and ten stamens, nine of which are conjoined at base.
Similar species: The scarce WOOD VETCH (*V. sylvatica*) is a trailing (up to 2 metres) perennial of the NYM, where it tends to be concentrated along the coastal fringe in wooded ravines, scrubland and sea cliffs. The hairless stems have ladder-like five to twenty opposing pairs of elliptical leaflets terminating in a branching tendril. The stipules are toothed. The long-stalked (from the leaf axils), scented flowers are a delicate lilac or white with blue or purple veins running through them. The flowers are longer (2–20mm) than in *V. hirsuta*, and five to twenty in number forming a single-sided spike. Flowers from June to August.

TOP AND INSET: GIANT BELLFLOWER. BELOW: HAIRY TARE.

▶ BROAD-LEAVED DOCK

Rumex obtusifolius
Family Polygonaceae

Flowering period: June to October.
Distribution: One of the most commonplace components of grassland plant communities.

Dock leaves are known by every child who has been stung by nettles as having a soothing antidote effect. It is a native perennial growing 60–120cm tall on roadsides, grassy places and waste ground. Upright, branching stems carry alternate leaves (up to 250mm long) that are long-stalked and broad oblong, tapering to a point, the underside veins slightly hairy. Lowermost leaves are heart-shaped at their base.

The inconspicuous hermaphrodite flowers are at first sight lacking in interest until looked at through a magnifier. These are numerous and form whorls around the upper stems. Flowers are 3mm, white and green but soon turning crimson, having a perianth with six lobes, 1–2mm, developing a swollen cork-like growth. The three inner are larger and triangular in shape with long teeth. There are six stamens and three stigma.
Similar species: CLUSTERED DOCK (*R. conglomeratus*) is less common with leaves that are round based, not heart-shaped as in *R. obtusifolius*. Flowers in leafy whorls almost to tip of stem. Grows alongside slow-moving water, or ponds.

▶ COMMON POPPY

Papaver rhoeas
Family Papaveraceae

Flowering period: June to August.
Distribution: A widely distributed arable weed throughout. Also known from the magnesian limestone band east of the Dales and South Yorkshire where it can be seen at the SFNR. Less frequent elsewhere. It is usually associated with soils having a pH value of 6.0–8.0. Very scarce in the Dales.

A native annual normally found close to settlements, where the bright red blooms make a welcome splash of colour on roadsides and disturbed ground. In the Wolds and VoY areas it often turns a whole field scarlet. The plant grows to 50cm in height, with roughly hairy branched stems. The latter carry leaves that are 25–160mm long, untoothed and narrow, the upper ones mostly stalkless, while the lower ones are stalked.

The stems carry solitary, paper-like flowers (70–100mm in diameter) which are hermaphrodite. These have four circular, overlapping petals with many bluish-black stamens and up to twelve stigmas forming a dark 'eye' to the bloom. The seed pods are almost round and hairless. Alternative names are corn rose and thunder flower. An infusion of the petals applied to the skin is said to reduce wrinkles.
Similar species: LONG-HEADED POPPY (*P. dubium*) shares a similar habitat but is considerably less common. It has paler flowers usually 30–70mm in diameter and absent the dark centre; with violet anthers. Stems have hairs closely pressed up to the stems and much longer seed pods. Flowering period June to August.

▶ BITTER VETCHLING

Lathyrus montanus
[Lathyrus linifolius]
Family Leguminosae

Flowering period: April to July.
Distribution: The most widespread member of the vetch family, common throughout the county.

This short (up to 40cm) perennial favours a dry situation on unimproved grasslands, railway cuttings, clifftops, roadsides and hedgerows on acid soils. It has winged, hairless stems carrying two to four pairs of long oval leaflets that are sometimes narrow lanceolate, terminating in a point rather than a tendril. The flowers (10–16mm long) are long-stalked and pea-like, arranged in pairs appearing reddish-purple fading to blue. The calyx is a dull purple-blue with prominent sepal teeth. The seed pods are a dull reddish through to black.
Similar species: COMMON VETCH (*Vicia sativa agg.*) is a short-medium (30–60cm) clambering annual sharing similar habitats as the bitter vetchling. Not all that common despite the name. It has similar, but larger (10–30mm) flowers that are reddish-purple and again grow in pairs, but in this case without a stalk. The leaves differ in being ladder-like with three to eight pairs of leaflets that can be oval or almost linear and end in a terminal tendril. Flowers from spring through to autumn.

TOP LEFT: BROAD-LEAVED DOCK. TOP RIGHT: COMMON POPPY. BELOW: BITTER VETCHLING.

❱ RED CLOVER
Trifolium pratense
Family Leguminosae

Flowering period: May to September.
Distribution: One of our most abundant and widespread plants. Found in all types of grassland except those on acid soils.

When given a free rein this variable native hairy perennial will reach 50cm. Trifoliate leaves are alternate with 10–30mm oval, slightly toothed leaflets, each often having an obvious white crescent marking. The lowest leaves are long-stalked. Flowers are hermaphrodite (12–15mm) forming globular or egg-shaped stalkless heads that are red or pinkish-purple, rarely white. There are five sepals with the lowest being the longest forming a tube. There are five petals, the lowest pair joined, upper petal the longest and side pairs overlapping. There are ten stamens with one stigma.
Similar species: See ZIG-ZAG CLOVER (*T. medium*).

❱ ZIG-ZAG CLOVER
Trifolium medium
Family Leguminosae

Flowering period: June to August.
Distribution: Though having a widespread distribution this species is nowhere as common as *T. pratense*.

Similar to red clover, but this native perennial is usually patch-forming. Typically found growing in hedgebanks, beside roads and on unimproved grasslands on richer soils. The straggling, often twisted, stems have given rise to the plant's common name. It may grow to 40cm with narrowly triangular stipules, not bristle-pointed.
  The sparsely hairy stems bear deep green leaves that are narrower than in red clover; untoothed but with fine hairs running along the margins. Flowers are 20mm in diameter, and are a rich reddish-purple showing whitish towards the centre. The base of the sepals is hairless.
Similar species: See RED CLOVER (*T. pratense*).

❱ GREAT BURNET
Sanguisorba officinalis
Family Rosaceae

Flowering period: June to September.
Distribution: Common on neutral to slightly base soils throughout the western Dales decreasing further east. In the North York Moors it is found around the periphery, with concentrations along the southern fringe. Also scattered through the Wolds and Vale of York. Absent from high peaks and moors.

This relation of the rose is a medium-tall (up to 1 metre) clump-forming hairless perennial of damp grasslands and road sides. The slightly branching stems carry attractive fern-like, pinnate leaves that are green above and grey beneath, with three to seven pairs of roundly toothed leaflets some 20–35mm in length. The hermaphrodite flowers are absent of petals, instead having deep red sepals that are tiny and forming a dense oblong head of some 10–20mm in length. This plant once had a use in stanching the flow of blood, hence the Latin name.
Similar species: None.

❱ SALAD BURNET
Sanguisorba minor
Family Rosaceae

Flowering period: May to September.
Distribution: Known from the Wolds, east coast and parts of the VoY. Also common in the western Dales, but less so on the magnesian limestones. In the NYM it is found along the coast and also concentrated along the southern fringes.

This is a short native perennial of the rose family preferring short grassland on calcareous soils, usually pastures, meadows, verges, rocky outcrops and in old quarries. It has deep roots that usually ensure the plant's survival in drought. The almost hairless stems grow to 30cm and carry four to twelve pairs of rounded, deeply-toothed leaflets, no longer than 20mm.
  This is a patch-forming plant with reddish flowers occurring in globular heads with feathery stigmas and green sepals instead of petals. Blooms are very attractive to insects and the leaves, if crushed, smell of cucumbers. Plant derives its name from the fact that it was once cultivated as a culinary herb.
Similar species: None.

TOP: ZIG-ZAG CLOVER. BELOW LEFT: GREAT BURNET. CENTRE: RED CLOVER. RIGHT: SALAD BURNET.

❯ MARSH CINQUEFOIL
Potentilla palustris
Family Rosaceae

Flowering period: May to July.
Distribution: This is an uncommon plant, but usually abundant where locally found. It has a scattered distribution in the Dales and on the magnesian limestones east of there and into the VoY. Also in the NYM, notably in Newtondale, the Esk Valley and Commondale. Scarce anywhere else.

This strikingly colourful flower is unusual among cinquefoils in not having yellow perianth members. It is a native hairless perennial, and forms an addition to the plant communities of wet grassland, marshes and lakesides. Growing to 40cm and often forming a ground covering carpet, it has long-stalked, pinnate leaves divided into up to seventeen pairs of toothed leaflets, together with a terminal leaflet.

The flowers, which grow in loose, forked clusters, are marked by their star-shape, formed from five deep wine-red or maroon oval sepals that are 10–15mm long. These taper to a point and separate the narrower and quite insignificant, deeper coloured petals. Bracts are present and spreading. The nectar from this flower is especially attractive to bees.
Similar species: None.

❯ HEDGE WOUNDWORT
Stachys sylvatica
Family Labiatae

Flowering period: June to September.
Distribution: Commonplace throughout the county as a colourful component of rough grassland, hedgerow bottoms and woodland margins in slightly shady situations.

The plant is roughly hairy, strong smelling and upright, with often-branching stems reaching heights of 120cm. The square stems bear opposing pairs of narrow spearhead-shaped or pointed oval leaves that are coarsely toothed, the lowermost stem leaves stalked. The plant gains its name from ancient uses of the leaves as poultices in healing wounds. Modern science seems to bear this out with the discovery that an antiseptic is contained within the plant's juice.

The hermaphrodite flowers, 13–18mm, are a deep beetroot red in colour with white blotches and streaks. They grow in a leafy spike forming whorls at the axils of the upper leaves. Five sepals are joined together into a calyx, the triangular teeth spreading and curving away from the corolla. The latter has five petals, with the upper two lobes hood-like in appearance, and the lower three bent backwards. There are four stamens and two stigmas.
Similar species: MARSH WOUNDWORT (*S. palustris*) is much less common, with only a peppering of sites in the North York Moors and Dales, and a slightly more widespread distribution on the magnesian limestones. It has stalkless or short-stalked, narrower lower stem leaves and pale pink flowers streaked with magenta. It grows by water and other damp places.

FIELD WOUNDWORT (*S. arvensis*) is rarer still. It grows up to 30cm with leaves that are rounder, more heart-shaped with blunt teeth. Flowers are a dull purple or pinkish colour with no prominent blotches or streaks. Flowers April to autumn.

❯ RED DEAD-NETTLE
Lamium purpureum
Family Labiatae

Flowering period: All year round.
Distribution: Very common throughout as an addition to grassy places, waste or disturbed ground, railway ballast and roadside verges. Absent from the high moors.

An aromatic annual related to the mints that, despite the name and similarity of appearance, is not related to the stinging nettle. This plant has robust upright and downy purplish stems reaching to a height of 45cm. Heart-shaped or oval leaves occur paired along the whole height of the stems and are stalked and bluntly-toothed. The young, uppermost leaves are often a dull purple-coloured.

Flowers are hermaphrodite red or purplish-pink, 10–17mm, forming whorled loose clusters at the base of the upper leaves. Five sepals are joined; five petals form a tube with two upper lobes being hood-like and the lower lobes divided and toothed.
Similar species: Almost as widespread, the COMMON HEMP-NETTLE (*Galeopsis tetrahit*) is a short-medium roughly hairy annual sharing similar habitats. It is a well-branched plant but

TOP: MARSH CINQUEFOIL. BELOW LEFT: RED DEAD-NETTLE. RIGHT: HEDGE WOUNDWORT.

with stalked leaves that are broadly lanceolate and toothed. Flowers are reddish-purple 10–20mm in whorls at base of upper leaves. Flowers July to September.

▶ BETONY
Stachys officinalis
Family Labiatae

Flowering period: June to October.
Distribution: Found throughout the lowlands on unmanaged grasslands, cliff-tops, meadows, open woods and roadsides.

Also called bishopswort, this medium hairy perennial is at home on soil substrates of all pH values. Growing to heights of up to 60cm, the stems carry opposite pairs of oblong, bluntly-toothed leaves, all of which are stalked but for the uppermost. The flowers occur at the end of the sparsely leaved stems.

Blooms are bell-shaped with a five-lobed calyx, bright reddish or purply-pink in colour, forming whorled, oblong spikes. As with other members of the dead-nettle family the flowers are attractive to bees. A physician to the Roman emperor Augustus claimed the plant could cure almost fifty medical complaints. The plant was also once thought to be a safeguard against witchcraft.
Similar species: Equally widespread, the COMMON HEMP-NETTLE (*Galeopsis tetrahit*) is a short-medium, roughly hairy annual sharing a similar habitat. It is a well-branched plant but with stalked leaves that are broadly lanceolate and toothed. Flowers are reddish-purple 10–20mm in whorls at base of upper leaves. Flowers from July to September.

▶ RED CAMPION
Silene dioica
Family Caryophyllaceae

Flowering period: May to June.
Distribution: Commonplace throughout except on acid soils and the high moors, though it is to be found around some reservoirs sited in the Pennines. Scarce on arable land.

An extremely abundant native biennial or perennial found on rich soils in woods, roadsides and hedge banks. It is a medium-tall (up to 100cm) plant with softly hairy, (sometimes sticky) branching stems carrying pointed oval leaves,

30–120mm untoothed and in opposite pairs, the lowest ones on winged stalks. Stipules are absent.

Flowers (18–25mm diameter) have a stalk-like base and are red or bright pink, less often white with an inner ring of white 'flaps'. The second part of the name, dioica, means 'two houses', and refers to the fact that male and female flowers are on different plants. There are five petals, each divided to half way, and five sepals joined to form a calyx with triangular, pointed teeth. The male flowers have ten stamens, the female ones five stigmas.
Similar species: None.

▶ SCARLET PIMPERNEL
Anagallis arvensis
Family Primulaceae

Flowering period: May to October.
Distribution: A widespread but infrequent arable weed found in the Wolds, VoY and the magnesian limestone corridor. Also found along the southern fringes of the NYM, near Great Ayton and along the coastal strip near Boulby. Also at SFNR in South Yorkshire, but rare in the Dales and absent from high moors.

This prostrate annual of calcareous soils is a pretty little flower, yet despite its bright colour can easily be overlooked on waste ground, in old quarries and (occasionally) on grassland. It is almost hairless with square stems of 6–35cm bearing pointed, oval or spear-shaped leaves 15–20mm long. These are black dotted on the under surface, unstalked and arranged in pairs or whorls.

The hermaphrodite flowers, also known as shepherd's weatherglass, are star-like 6–14mm across and usually rich scarlet, but sometimes pink or blue. They are solitary, long-stalked at base of leaves, and only open in the morning, closing again in the afternoon or if overcast. Petals are five in number, blunt and slightly toothed at tip with hairs along the margins. There are five narrow-pointed sepals, five stamens and one stigma.
Similar species: None.

▶ BILBERRY
Vaccinium myrtillus
Family Ericaceae

Flowering period: April to August.
Distribution: Very abundant component of upland moors, the edge of forest rides and in open

TOP LEFT: BETONY. TOP RIGHT: RED CAMPION. MIDDLE: SCARLET PIMPERNEL. BELOW: BILBERRY.

woodland on acid subsoils; often growing in combination with heather. Sometimes found at lower altitudes where suitable soils persist. Absent or very rare elsewhere.

This is one of six species of bilberry indigenous to Britain. It is a hairless deciduous undershrub growing to 60cm with acutely-angled green stems carrying bright green, finely serrated oval leaves (10–30mm) alternately arranged. The nodding, globular hermaphrodite flowers are red, dark pink or greenish-pink and grow singly or in pairs from the leaf axil. Bracts are scale-like and there are four to five sepals, joined to form a slightly lobed calyx. Petals (4–6mm) are four to five in number, joined to form an ovoid globe with the white petal tips turned back. There are eight to ten stamens and one stigma.

The dark glossy black fruit are a favourite for making tarts and preserves, while a traditional Yorkshire dessert made from the fruit is known as 'mucky-mouth pie'.
Similar species: None.

▶ EUROPEAN LARCH
Larix decidua
Family Pinaceae

Flowering period: March to April.
Distribution: A seventeenth century introduction, this now widespread deciduous conifer is found in commercial forests and a few wild situations. This pyramidal tree is often planted as a 'nurse' crop for other broad-leaved species.

Mature specimens often form a significant feature of the landscape, with new growth giving a vibrant green in springtime, while the gold of autumn adds to the pleasure of this season. It grows to heights of almost fifteen metres with rough, grey-brown bark. The leaves are pale green, single (less than 1 mm wide) and form a tufted rosette, almost feathery and pleasantly scented. Male flowers (10mm across) resemble a short yellow catkin, while female blooms (slightly larger than the males) are bright red and look like small cones. The fruit forms a woody, egg-shaped cone growing along the branches.
Similar Species: None

▶ BLOODY CRANESBILL
Geranium sanguineum
Family Geraniaceae

Flowering period: June to August.
Distribution: Very rare in the NYM. More common on the magnesian limestone belt and in the Dales. Elsewhere localized but far from common.

Bloody cranesbill is not an expletive but the description of a pretty perennial preferring dry grassy places on limestone pavements and rocky outcrops. It grows to heights of 30cm having hairy stems and leaves that are palmate and deeply divided almost to the base. Leaves have finely toothed margins. The stems carry five-petalled blooms 25–30mm across. These have a delicate appearance, as if made from crepe paper, and are a rich red magenta or pink, less commonly white, veined with darker purple.
Similar species: None.

▶ FUCHSIA
Fuchsia magellanica
Family Onagraceae

Flowering period: June to September.
Distribution: A plant introduced from Chile and found wild as a garden escape in scattered locations throughout the county, preferring the semi-shade of light woodland or hedgebanks.

Growing to heights of up to 3 metres, this deciduous or evergreen shrub has pretty flowers also known as 'lady's eardrops' that are likened to a ballerina in a tutu. It forms a rounded bush with gracefully arching reddish stems. These carry dark green oval to lanceolate leaves (up to 3–5cm long) with serrated margins, either in opposite pairs or whorls of three to five. The leaves have prominent red veins.

The bell-shaped hermaphrodite flowers (4–10cm) hang from the leaf axils on reddish stalks equal in length to the flower. The latter are drooping and have four long but slender, bright red sepals and four shorter but broad, purple petals. There are eight long-protruding stamens with purple anthers.
Similar species: None.

TOP AND INSET: BLOODY CRANESBILL. BELOW LEFT: FUCHSIA. RIGHT: EUROPEAN LARCH.

❱ HEATHER
Calluna vulgaris
Family Ericaceae

Flowering period: July through to September.
Distribution: One of the most widespread components of northern moorlands. Very common from woodland fringes, along roadsides and the drier parts of acid moors and heaths of the NYM, parts of the Dales, and the Pennines of South and West Yorkshire. Also known from lowland sites where suitable habitat exists.

This short to medium (to 60cm) height evergreen undershrub, commonly known as ling, has paired leaves (1–2mm) closely packed in opposite rows on woody stems. Flowers (3–5mm) are hermaphrodite and pink or reddish-purple in leafy stalked spikes 30–150mm long. Four petals are joined to form a bell with one stigma and eight stamens. The four pointed sepals are longer than the petals.
Similar species: CROSS-LEAVED HEATH (*Erica tetralix*) is less common in the Dales. A downy undershrub favouring wetter areas of acid soils on heaths, peaty moors, flushes and bogs. Differs from *C. vulgaris* in having linear leaves arranged in whorls of four, fringed with hairs, and larger (6–7mm) globular-shaped pale pink flowers forming compact heads from June onwards.

   BELL HEATHER (*Erica cinerea*) is a short and wiry evergreen undershrub growing to 40cm on acid substrates. It differs from *E. tetralix* in being hairless and growing on drier areas of heaths. Has nodding reddish-purple flowers in stalked spikes and leaves arranged in whorls of three. Flowering from July to September.

❱ COMMON MALLOW
Malva sylvestris
Family Malvaceae

Flowering period: June to October.
Distribution: Found on the magnesian limestones, less so along the Wolds, east coast and VoY. Very rare in the Dales and elsewhere in the county.

This variable, slightly hairy perennial is a plant of uncultivated niches – waysides, along riverbanks and in waste places. It grows to 50cm with palmately lobed leaves having seven fingers. These grow either from the base or are spirally arranged up the stem. Leaves sometimes have a dark spot, are 50–100mm long with rounded teeth. The 25–40mm flowers are hermaphrodite. There are usually two or more together, pale to dark pink with five slightly notched petals with dark stripes. The ring of triangular sepals, five in total, are not joined at their base. The stamens are numerous and form a prominent club-like head imparting to the bloom the appearance of a small hibiscus flower.
Similar species: MUSK MALLOW (*M. moschata*) is considerably rarer with a scattering of instances on the magnesian limestones, NYM, and in West and South Yorkshire. Extremely rare in the Dales. An equally attractive plant with solitary flowers on sparsely hairy stalks. Leaves are alternate, 50–80mm with three to seven toothed lobes, the lower leaves kidney-shaped with long stalks, uppermost leaves short-stemmed. Flowerheads are larger (40–60mm) than *M. sylvestris*, with five delicate pink or lilac, deeply-cut petals with crimson veins. It flowers June to August in unmanaged grassland on calcareous soils.

❱ THRIFT
Armeria maritima
Family Plumbaginaceae

Flowering period: April to August.
Distribution: Known from locations along the east coast. Though normally a maritime plant it has also been recorded from the high limestone fells of Teesdale, with one reported instance in Wensleydale.

Thrift, or sea pink, is a low, downy and cushion-forming perennial preferring sea cliffs and rocky crevices and grassy slopes close to the coast. The plant has 20–150mm long leaves being linear and not unlike those of cultivated chives. The hermaphrodite flowers are long-stalked (10–15mm) and slightly fragrant, dark or pale pink, having rounded heads 7–12mm with a brown bract and sepal teeth with short bristles. The individual florets have five sepals forming a delicate, paper-like calyx with five hairy ribs, five stamens and an equal number of stigmas.
Similar species: None.

TOP LEFT: HEATHER. TOP RIGHT: COMMON MALLOW. BELOW: THRIFT.

▶ INDIAN BALSAM

Impatiens glandulifera
Family Balsaminaceae

Flowering period: July to October.
Distribution: Introduced as a garden plant from the Himalayas in 1839 and first recorded in the wild sixteen years later. Very common in West Yorkshire, South Yorkshire and on the magnesian limestones, but less common everywhere else.

Also called Himalayan balsam, or policeman's helmet, this attractive relative of busy Lizzie is especially invasive. It favours damp ground alongside streams and rivers. The plant's successful colonization is entirely due to its efficient seed dispersal mechanism, which can explosively discharge them up to 12 metres. Each plant produces over 2,000 seeds.

The short-stalked leaves are pointed oval or heart-shaped, slightly toothed and 60–180mm long. The pretty, snapdragon-like pale to dark pink blooms are carried on tall (1.5 metre) fleshy stems, hairless and often red-tinged. The hermaphrodite flowers, 24–40mm, grow on slender stems grouped five to six from the leaf base. Flowers have a short spur and five petals, two joined each side and the uppermost forming a broad hood. There are five stamens and one stigma.
Similar species: None.

▶ ROSEBAY WILLOWHERB

Epilobium angustifolium
Family Onagraceae

Flowering period: July to September.
Distribution: Very widespread throughout in waste places, roadside verges, railway embankments, rubbish tips, heaths and unmanaged grassland. Also an early colonizer of cleared woodland.

Sometimes known as fireweed because it favours ground that has been burnt, this native patch-forming perennial grows up to 1.5 metres tall. It was a popular garden flower during Victorian times, and was also the first species to re-colonize London sites bombed during World War II. The upright, slightly reddish, hairless stems have lanceolate, slightly toothed leaves arranged alternately up their length.

Forming a loose spike, the hermaphrodite flowers are 20–30mm diameter. Each has four prominent dark purple sepals and four bright purple-pink petals, unequal and slightly notched, or not at all, with eight stamens and four lobed stigmas. After flowering, the white silky-plumed seeds are a commonplace sight drifting on the autumn wind.
Similar species: See GREAT HAIRY WILLOWHERB (*E. hirsutum*).

▶ GREAT HAIRY WILLOWHERB

Epilobium hirsutum
Family Onagraceae

Flowering period: July to August.
Distribution: Almost, but not quite as common as *E. angustifolium* in wet places along canal sides, riverbanks, ditches or ungrazed and waste ground.

In some areas also known as 'codlins and cream', this tall (up to 2 metres) softly hairy native perennial becomes branched at leaf axils near the top. The leaves (75–125mm long) are stalkless, pointed lanceolate with serrated margins, and are slightly hairy giving them a greyish tinge,. They are arranged in opposite pairs clasping the stem.

The flowers are larger than either broad-leaved or rosebay willowherb and grow in loose clusters appearing from the head of the plant. There are four notched petals, 15–25mm across, bright pink or purply-pink with white centres. The prominent stigma is four-lobed and white.
Similar species: See ROSEBAY WILLOWHERB (*E. angustifolium*).

▶ BROAD-LEAVED WILLOWHERB

Epilobium montanum agg.
Family Onagraceae

Flowering period: June to August.
Distribution: Very common and about as widely distributed as *E. angustifolium*. A plant of waste ground, waysides, hedgerows, walls, ditches and open grassland. Absent from moorlands.

It is a native perennial growing to heights of 50cm with scaly rounded stems that are reddish tinged. The 40–80mm long leaves are broad, lanceolate and toothed, arranged mostly in opposite pairs, but occasionally in threes. They are very short-stalked. The flowers are hermaphrodite and pink, some 6–9mm across, appearing in an elongated inflorescence. Four equal petals are obviously notched with eight stamens and a four-lobed stigma.

TOP: INDIAN BALSAM. LEFT: ROSEBAY WILLOWHERB. RIGHT: BROAD-LEAVED WILLOWHERB. BELOW: GREAT HAIRY WILLOWHERB.

Similar species: MARSH WILLOWHERB
(*E. palustre*) is rare on magnesian limestone, in the
VoY and the Wolds. Very prolific in the NYM and
on the moorlands of the western Dales and South
Yorkshire. A plant of damp places growing to
50cm tall. The hairless stems carry opposite pairs
of narrow unstalked lanceolate leaves that may be
scarcely toothed or not and are three times longer
than they are broad. The 4–6mm delicate pink,
occasionally white, flowers have four equal petals
that are deeply notched and grow in a drooping
posture singly on short stalks. Flowers from July
to August.

❯ FIELD BINDWEED
Convolvulus arvensis
Family Convolvulaceae

Flowering period: June to September.
Distribution: Common along the magnesian
limestone belt but tailing off west of there towards
the Dales. Less frequent in the NYM and mostly
concentrated along the southern fringe and down
the east coast. Infrequent in the Wolds and
elsewhere.

Growing to 2 metres, this creeping and twining
native perennial is a common addition to plant
communities in waste places and along roadsides.
The slightly downy stems twine anti-clockwise
and carry 20–50mm long, arrow-shaped leaves
arranged spirally up the stems.
    The hermaphrodite flowers (15–30mm)
appear solitary or in small clusters. They have
delicately shaded pastel pink petals that are
pleated and forming a shallow, flaring corona.
Petals are banded with white. There are five sepals
joined at base, five stamens and two stigmas.
Similar species: SEA BINDWEED (*Calystegia
soldanella*) is considerably scarcer, known from a
few locations along the east coast, at Spurn Head
and Ruswarp. It is a prostrate creeping perennial
preferring sand and shingle habitats. The hairless
stems carry long-stalked kidney-shaped leaves and
larger (40–50mm) flowers that are pink with white
stripes. The bracts are shorter than the sepals.
Flowers June to September.

❯ PINK PURSLANE
Montia sibirica
Family Portulacaceae

Flowering period: April to July.
Distribution: A garden escape introduced from the
USA and which has since become established
though not so widely distributed. There are
scattered instances throughout the Dales, on the
magnesian limestones and in the NYM.

This attractive fleshy plant is a component of
lowland habitats frequenting damp woods,
streamsides and occasionally roadsides and lanes.
The quite delicate, hairless stems grow to heights
of 30cm. Leaves are 2–3cm long, heart-shaped, or
pointed oval, with the lowermost long-stalked and
stem leaves growing in opposite, stalkless pairs
from which the long-stalked flowers appear.
Flowers are 10–20mm diameter and have five
obviously notched petals, 4–8mm, that are pink or
whitish with pink margins and darker streaks. The
anthers are a prominent red.
Similar species: None.

❯ WILD PINK
Dianthus plumarius
Family Caryophyllaceae

Flowering period: June to August.
Distribution: Extremely rare. Colonies of this pretty
flower have long been established on the ruins of
Fountains Abbey, a surviving relict from the
personal gardens of the resident Cistercian monks.

Growing to heights of 30cm, this tufted plant is
hairless with narrow, lanceolate, rough-edged
leaves growing in opposite pairs. The pretty,
fragrant flowers are either solitary or grow in lax
clusters, and may be pale pink or white with five
petals, the latter divided halfway into the feathery
lobes giving them a ragged appearance. The calyx
is up to 15mm in length with two to four pointed
segments up to one third the length of the tube.
Similar species: None.

❯ DEPTFORD PINK
Dianthus armeria
Family Caryophyllaceae

Flowering period: June to August.
Distribution: Extremely rare. A plant normally
associated with the south of Britain. It was found
on derelict ground near the river Aire in West

TOP: FIELD BINDWEED. CENTRE LEFT: WILD PINK. RIGHT: PINK PURSLANE. BELOW: DEPTFORD PINK.

Yorkshire. How the plant came to be here is uncertain, although almost certainly it was an introduction.

This stiffly hairy, greyish-green biennial is a plant of dry places and disturbed ground growing to heights up to 60cm. The stems grow from a basal rosette of spoon-shaped, pale green lanceolate leaves. Stem leaves are pointed linear, keeled and sheathed at the base.

The flowers (8–15mm) have five petals that are bright pink or rose-red. They have toothed edges and are often delicately spotted and resembling a small garden sweet William. Blooms are stalkless and occur in a tight inflorescence of two to ten flat flowerheads, surrounded by upward pointing green calyx. The sepal tube is softly hairy.
Similar species: none.

◗ COMMON STORKSBILL
Erodium cicutarium
Family Geraniaceae

Flowering period: April to September.
Distribution: Scarcely distributed along the magnesian limestone corridor, in the NYM and down the east coast. Extremely rare in the Dales. Also known from Skipwith Common in the VoY.

This low-medium annual/biennial is normally found on bare and grassy ground. The slender, creeping stems, up to 100cm, are stickily hairy and carry pairs of pinnate leaves 20–200mm long with deeply-lobed leaflets and lanceolate stipules.

Flowers, 8–18mm, are hermaphrodite and grow in umbel-like heads with up to ten flowers. The latter have five oval, pointed pink or purplish-pink petals (sometimes white), five stamens and five stigmas. Petals are often uneven and are easily shed. The long pointed capsule is likened to the bill of a stork.
Similar species: None.

◗ HERB ROBERT
Geranium robertianum
Family Geraniaceae

Flowering period: April to November.
Distribution: Extremely common herb throughout the county in open grassland, woods, on walls, stony places and shady hedgebanks.

A strong-smelling plant that appears to flower intermittently any time of year, this annual or biennial grows up to 50cm tall. The branched stems are quite brittle and carry leaves of 15–60mm from the base of plant, or in pairs, each deeply divided into three to five irregularly toothed lobes. Stems are hairy below, less so higher up. Sunshine usually turns both stems and leaves an attractive crimson colour.

The 20mm diameter hermaphrodites have five scarcely notched pink petals streaked with white. These form loose clusters of two to five stalked blooms. There are five bristle-tipped, oval sepals of 7–9mm length, and ten orange or purple stamens and five slender stigmas.
Similar species: SHINING CRANESBILL (*G. lucidum*) is a frequent find on walls, hedgebanks and humus-filled niches in rocky places, usually on lime. Scarce in the NYM. Growing to a height of 30cm this practically hairless plant can be easily identified by its glossy red, palmate leaves. These are toothed, cut to about halfway and have a waxy feel. Stems sometimes redden with exposure to the sun. The 10–15mm diameter flowers have five un-notched white-streaked pink petals. Flowers May to August.

HEDGEROW CRANESBILL (*G. pyrenaicum*) is scarcer. Also known as mountain cranesbill despite not being an upland species. It is a perennial garden escape that has colonized roadsides and waste places near habitation. The leaves are cut to about halfway. Flowers are pinky-purple or mauve-pink, 15mm across with well notched petals, appearing from May to September.

◗ CUT-LEAVED CRANESBILL
Geranium dissectum
Family Geraniaceae

Flowering period: May to September.
Distribution: As common as *G. lucidum*, but less frequent in the Dales and more widely found on the magnesian limestones. In the NYM it is scattered and not so common.

A short-medium (up to 50cm tall) native annual or biennial of waste places, open grassland, bridleways and tracks. The principal distinguishing feature is the finely divided leaves cut almost to their base, carried on branching, hairy stems, the hairs turned back. Leaves are paired either side of the straggling stems and are 20–70mm long, carried on long stalks near base of

TOP AND INSET: HERB ROBERT. LEFT: CUT-LEAVED CRANESBILL. RIGHT: COMMON STORKSBILL.

plant, becoming shorter further up the stem. Flowers occur singly or are paired from the leaf base and are 8mm across and pink or reddish-pink with five 4–5mm equal petals that are oval and notched. Bracts are slender. There are ten stamens and half as many slender stigmas.
Similar species: None.

▶ SAINFOIN
Onobrychis viciifolia
Family Leguminosae

Flowering period: June to September.
Distribution: This native perennial was introduced from France in the seventeenth century and is somewhat scarce. Confined only to scattered locations in dry grassland along the magnesian limestone belt east of Leeds.

Growing to heights up 80cm this relative of the humble pea has sparsely hairy, upright branching stems carrying alternate pinnate leaves with from six to fourteen pairs of oblong or linear untoothed leaflets (10–30mm long) plus a terminal leaf. The leaf stalk is short.

The attractive flower (10–12mm), up to fifty in number, forms a dense and downy, lupin-like terminal spike growing from leaf axil, the lowermost petals being rich pink, the upper ones paler with red or purple veins. Flowers are hermaphrodite having ten stamens and one stigma. It produces fruit in the form of short, flattened seed pods. Five sepals are joined in a calyx having long, slender-pointed teeth, sometimes red-tinged.
Similar species: None.

▶ REST-HARROW
Ononis repens
Family Leguminosae

Flowering period: July to September.
Distribution: Confined to calcareous terrain but scarce everywhere, except the magnesian limestone corridor where distribution is slightly more common.

This robust, pretty pink member of the pea family is thus named on account of its tenacious and matted underground stems which would foul up the ox-drawn ploughs of old. Of short-medium height (30–70cm), this stickily hairy perennial undershrub, is sometimes softly spined and has leaf-like bracts.

Leaves (up to 20mm) are alternately arranged, trefoliate with blunt or slightly notched oval leaflets, the latter lightly toothed. The pea-like flowers (10–15mm) grow from the leaf axils in leafy stalked spikes and are pink, sometimes softly streaked white. In shape the wings equal the keel in length.
Similar species: SPINY REST-HARROW (*O. spinosa*) is considerably rarer. It is a more erect plant with robust, spine-tipped stems. Distinguished by two lines of hairs, instead of being hairy all around, and leaves are never notched. Favours a similar habitat and flowering period.

▶ COMMON FUMITORY
Fumaria officinalis agg.
Family Berberidaceae

Flowering period: April to autumn.
Distribution: A fairly widespread plant of the magnesian limestone belt, but less common elsewhere to the point of being very rare in the Dales. Infrequent along the Holderness coast and in the VoY.

A native plant that readily colonizes disturbed roadsides and waste ground on base soils. It is a hairless annual scrambling to heights of 40cm, with grey-green branching stems carrying somewhat flimsy, stalked leaves 20–100mm. These are arranged spirally and are divided into narrow lobes that are oblong or spear-shaped.

The tiny pink hermaphrodite flowers, 7–9mm, are elongated and darker tipped, ten to forty in number forming a crowded spike. Sepals are more than a quarter the length of petals 2–3mm long and toothed at the base. Four unequal petals are held close together, both inner petals obscured by larger, outer petals. There are two stamens and a two-lobed stigma.
Similar species: RAMPING FUMITORY (*F. capreolata*) is so rare it has only been recorded from one location in the Craven area of the Dales, though known from a few more sites along the coast of the NYM. It has stems up to one metre carrying flowers 10–14mm that are white tipped with reddish-pink, with around twenty in the inflorescence. It flowers between May and September and favours a hedgerow habitat.

TOP: SAINFOIN. RIGHT: REST-HARROW. BELOW: COMMON FUMITORY.

❱ COMMON BISTORT
Polygonum bistorta
Family Polygonaceae

Flowering period: June to October.
Distribution: Common throughout the Dales but less so in the magnesian belt to the east. Has a moderately scattered distribution in the NYM, where it can be seen in Eskdale, Cropton, Rosedale, Farndale and Sleights.

A scarcely hairy perennial of upland meadows, damp grassland and roadsides. Also called snakeroot, this patch-forming plant grows to heights of 100cm, and provides areas of pink to meadows full of yellow buttercups. When occurring in quantity it gives off an unpleasant smell reminiscent of dog faeces. An unbranched erect stem has leaves that are lanceolate with winged stalks in alternate pairs, become smaller to non-existent up the stem.

Pink flowers form densely-packed spikes up to 15mm diameter and 100mm in length that from a distance can be mistaken for common spotted orchid. In a Dales recipe called Ledger Pudding bistort was the principal ingredient, mixed with other fresh, edible wild plants and hard-boiled eggs.

Similar species: AMPHIBIOUS BISTORT (*P. amphibium*) is quite scarce in NYM and the Dales, increasing into the magnesian corridor. It is found in the Washburn Valley of West Yorkshire and in the wetlands of the VoY. An attractive creeping perennial with both aqueous and terrestrial forms. The former is a floating plant that roots at the leaf axils with leaves not tapering at the base; the second form is smaller, more upright, hairy and with longer and thinner leaves. Flowers in both cases form dense pink spikes, usually from June to September in still or slow-moving fresh water, or along the margins in the case of the terrestrial form.

ALPINE BISTORT (*P. viviparum*) is very rare, growing in lowland grasslands in Teesdale, a handful of sites in the Three Peaks area and in upper Wharfedale. It is a short (up to 30cm), hairless perennial with narrow, tapering lanceolate leaves. Upright spikes have white or pale pink flowers and red bulbils at the base. Flowers June to August.

❱ REDSHANK
Polygonum persicaria [Persicaria maculosa]
Family Polygonaceae

Flowering period: June to October or until killed by frost.
Distribution: Widespread native annual more common to the lowlands of the NYM and magnesian limestone. Scattered elsewhere in suitable habitats of the VoY and southern Wolds.

Both terrestrial and amphibious forms are recorded. It is plant of waste, arable or open ground, waysides, marshes and wet meadows, also slow-moving streams. It can survive on most soils but prefers rich and peaty acid soils. A sprawling, almost hairless plant, this member of the knotweed family has fleshy, red-tinged branching stems up to 90cm tall, with alternate 50–150mm long lanceolate leaves that are untoothed and tapering towards the base, sometimes dark-spotted. The dark spot is, according to folklore, attributed to the devil.

The numerous flowers are hermaphrodite, each 3–6mm long and forming densely packed elongated spikes similar to bistort. Flowers may be pink, red or rarely white. Each flower has five petal-like parts to the perianth, eight stamens and two or three stigmas. This is one of the first plants to germinate after topsoil is relocated.

Similar species: AMPHIBIOUS BISTORT (*P. amphibium*).

❱ BIRDSEYE PRIMROSE
Primula farinosa
Family Primulaceae

Flowering period: May to July.
Distribution: A nationally rare plant only existing at this specific latitude on calcareous soils. It is reasonably commonplace in the Dales, and Teesdale, but becomes much less so further east. In the NYM it is considered a species at risk, only occurring at a handful of widely scattered sites, one being Rydale.

This is one of my favourite flowers, a strikingly pretty native perennial that may be found on damp grassland, flushes and riversides, and also in some abundance on the better drained calcareous pastures of the Three Peaks, notably those surrounding Ingleborough between 280 and 390 metres altitude.

A single stem rises to heights of 15cm from a

TOP LEFT: COMMON BISTORT. RIGHT: REDSHANK. BELOW: BIRDSEYE PRIMROSE.

rosette of spoon-shaped toothed leaves, the stem and underside of the leaves commonly a mealy white. The stems carry a loose head (three to twelve in number) of rich candy pink flowers each with a bright yellow eye in the centre. Flowers have flat heads, are 10–15mm across, each with five heart-shaped, notched petals. Sepal teeth are pointed.
Similar species: None.

▶ LESSER SKULLCAP
Scutellaria minor
Family Labiatae

Flowering period: July to October.
Distribution: Very rare. Known from only two sites, one in West Yorkshire, the other on the western fringe of the Dales.

A native perennial of wet heaths, this is a delicate low (up to 10cm) creeping plant often overlooked in taller grass and sedge communities. Sometimes hairy, it has leaves in opposite pairs varying from oval to lanceolate in form and barely toothed. The two-lipped flowers are pale pink or pinkish-purple spotted darker. These grow singly or in pairs from the leaf axils. The corolla is almost straight, the lower lobe sometimes turned down.
Similar species: None.

▶ COMMON HEMP-NETTLE
Galeopsis tetrahit
Family Labiatae

Flowering period: July to September.
Distribution: Widespread and common throughout the NYM on verges, waste ground and field margins. Also abundant on the magnesian limestones, but scarcer in the Dales and everywhere else.

This member of the mint family is a roughly hairy native annual growing up to 100cm in height. The leaves are 30–100mm long and nettle-like, pointed oval with toothed edges, and paired on the well-branched, upright stems. The leaf stalk is usually shorter than the leaf. Stems often have swellings immediately beneath the leaf node.
    It has hermaphrodite flowers, 15–30mm, growing in whorls at the base of the upper leaves. They have five petals with the upper ones hood-like and pink (rarely yellow or white) spotted or striped with darker pink. Each flower has five

sepals forming a tubular calyx tipped with spines.
Similar species: See RED DEAD NETTLE (*Lamium purporeum*) and BETONY (*Stachys officinalis*).

▶ WATER MINT
Mentha aquatica
Family Labiatae

Flowering period: July to September.
Distribution: Commonplace throughout the NYM, the Dales and on the magnesian limestone belt, favouring marshland, stream banks, rivers, ponds, reservoirs, wet meadows and alder carr. Absent from high moors and rare in urban areas.

A wonderfully aromatic perennial herb. Growing to heights of 80cm this purply-hairy plant has square stems that carry 20–100mm paired leaves that are pointed oval, toothed and short-stalked. The leaves of this plant can be used to make a refreshing tea infusion. The flowerheads are pink or pinkish-lilac and grow in many, short-stalked clusters from the base of the upper leaves, as well as in a rounded terminal head.
    Flowers are hermaphrodite, 5–10mm, with five petals forming a corona, the upper two almost joined, the lowest three lobes being a touch larger. There are five sepals, 2.5–4mm, in a long-toothed calyx that is softly hairy with up to thirteen veins; four protruding stamens and two stigmas. Sometimes forms a hybrid with *M. arvensis*.
Similar species: None.

▶ CORN MINT
Mentha arvensis
Family Labiatae

Flowering period: May to October.
Distribution: Much rarer than *M. aquatica* with only a peppering of sites in NYM and on the magnesian limestones. Even less frequent in the Dales.

This medium hairy perennial can be found on waste and disturbed ground, field margins and grassland. It grows to heights of 60cm and has pointed oval, short-stalked toothed leaves. The flowers are pinky-lilac and grow in 10–18mm whorls from the base of the leaves all along the length of the stalk. Lacking the terminal flowerhead of corn mint. The calyx tube is hairy and short-toothed.
Similar species: See SPEAR MINT (*M. spicata*).

TOP LEFT: LESSER SKULLCAP. TOP RIGHT: COMMON HEMP-NETTLE. BELOW LEFT: WATER MINT. RIGHT: CORN MINT.

❱ SPEAR MINT
Mentha spicata
Family Labiatae

Flowering period: July to October.
Distribution: A widespread but sparse garden herb that has escaped and established itself in the wild throughout on waste ground, stream bankings and roadside verges close to habitation.

This is a short-medium height perennial that can be either hairy or hairless. Growing to heights of 60cm, its oval leaves are toothed and arranged in opposite, unstalked pairs and may be dark green or greyish, wrinkled and shiny. The arrow-shaped lilac pink flowers grow in short spikes from the axils of the upper leaves and also in a longer terminal inflorescence.
Similar species: see CORN MINT (*M. arvensis*)

❱ MOUNTAIN EVERLASTING
Antennaria dioica
Family Compositae

Flowering period: June to July.
Distribution: Rare. This plant occurs in a handful of sites in the NYM – Caydale, Farndale and others – and also in the Three Peaks area of the Dales where it is a montane species slightly more common than in the east.

A low-short creeping native perennial with rooting runners, alternatively known by the name of cat's paw or cat's foot because of the appearance of the tight cluster of the male flowerheads enclosed by light, papery bracts. Usually growing to 20cm, the stem rises erect from a basal rosette. Leaves are woolly beneath, those of the rosette being oval and broadest at the tip. Stem leaves are upright, lanceolate and alternately arranged close to the stem.
 Male and female flowers are found on separate plants, the male being 8–12mm diameter and resembling a daisy with a pink centre, while female flowers are 5–7mm and like small brushes. These have two to eight pink or red flowers lacking rays forming terminal clusters (umbels), with sepal-like bracts that are white or pink. It can grow at any altitude and favours short mountain grasslands and humus-filled niches in rocks on less base-rich soils.
Similar species: None.

❱ BUTTERBUR
Petasites hybridus
Family Compositae

Flowering period: February to April.
Distribution: Fairly common throughout. Large colonies are to be seen in the Forge Valley west of Scarborough.

The unusual pink flower spikes of this patch-forming native perennial push through the ground in early springtime, about a month before the leaves dominate the summer bankings of streams, damp places and roadsides. The rounded and toothed, rhubarb-like leaves of this plant are a pale green colour, hairy beneath and can grow to as much as 90cm across, sprouting from underground stems usually after the flowers have died back.
 There are male and female flowers on separate plants. Flowers appear as a solitary cluster on scaly, robust stems some 10–80cm tall. Purplish-pink or lilac flowerheads are brush-like and rayless formed from tiny florets encompassed by rows of strap-like bracts. There are five petals forming a tube, with hair-like sepals, five stamens and one stigma. The large leaves were once used by country dairies to wrap pats of butter, hence the name.
Similar species: As its name suggests WINTER HELIOTROPE (*P. fragrans*) is a plant that turns to face the sun as the latter progresses across the sky. It is a much scarcer plant – a garden escape introduced in the early nineteenth century from the Mediterranean – that has established itself along roadsides and waste ground. Very rare in the Dales. In the NYM it is a little more frequent along the coastal fringe.
 The plant is a perennial and shorter (up to 20cm) than *P. hybridus*, with smaller (20cm across), bright green leaves that are roundish, slightly serrated and leathery. There are fewer, brush-like pink or lilac flowers, both blooms and leaves appearing together from March to May.

❱ MARSH VALERIAN
Valeriana dioica
Family Valerianaceae

Flowering period: May to June.
Distribution: Very abundant in both the NYM and the Dales, less so on the magnesian limestones and the Wolds. Rare elsewhere.

TOP LEFT: MOUNTAIN EVERLASTING. RIGHT: MARSH VALERIAN. BELOW LEFT: BUTTERBUR. RIGHT: SPEAR MINT.

A short (up to 45cm), practically hairless native perennial of flushes, marshland and fen. It possesses creeping runners, from which root leaves are long-stalked oval, and untoothed. Stem leaves are pinnately lobed, unstalked with six to eight pairs of leaflets plus a terminal leaflet.

It is easier to distinguish from common valerian since the latter has tighter, brighter pink flower clusters. The pale pink or white flowers have five petals and form short-stalked, rounded clusters from the axils of the upper leaves. Stamens and styles exist on separate male and female plants.

Similar species: COMMON VALERIAN (*V. officinalis*) grows much taller, up to 1.2 metres, and is often mistaken for a member of the carrot family (*umbelliferae*). It is a native perennial of riversides, marshes and tall grassland communities. Usually the plant is unbranched, with a hairy lower stem. Leaves are pinnate, the lowermost stalked and leaflets toothed and lanceolate. Dark pink flowers form a tightly packed rounded inflorescence.

▶ RAGGED ROBIN
Lychnis flos-cuculi
Family Caryophyllaceae

Flowering period: May to August.
Distribution: Very common throughout the region, especially in the Dales and NYM. Not quite as frequent in the Wolds and VoY due to loss of suitable habitat, but Askham Bog near York has some especially impressive swathes. Infrequent on the magnesian limestones. Found in a few locations in West and South Yorkshire.

An unusual flower having the appearance of a shredded red campion. The second half of the name means 'flower of the cuckoo'. The favoured habitat is nutrient-deficient ground, such as damp meadows, marshes, drainage ditches and the edge of ponds. This medium-tall (not more than 90cm) upright native perennial has basal leaves that are stalked and oblong, from which rises a rough, reddish stem. The upper leaves are light green, grass-like and lanceolate in opposite pairs, each pair being joined and clasping the stem.

The slightly branching stems carry the bright pink hermaphrodite flowers solitary or in loose clusters of two to four blooms having widely spread heads 25–40mm across. There are five petals deeply divided into four linear lobes, five reddish sepals joined into a calyx, ten stamens and five stigmas. This plant is loved by bumblebees and several species of butterfly.
Similar species: None.

▶ FOXGLOVE
Digitalis purpurea
Family Scrophulariaceae

Flowering period: June to September.
Distribution: This handsome plant is widespread and commonplace throughout on rail and roadside embankments, hedgerows, scrub, waste ground, woods, waste places and heaths.

A member of the figwort group of plants, this spectacular native perennial or biennial prefers acidic soils and grows anything up to 1.5 metres in height. It is a downy plant, unbranched with broad, lanceolate leaves (150–300mm long) that are wrinkled and round-toothed. The lower leaves form a rosette while the upper ones spiral up the stem.

The hermaphrodite flowers form a spectacular tapering spike. Individual flowers are up to 50mm long, pink or purple, less commonly white. Each has five short sepals and five petals joined as a flaring tube with twin lips fringed with white. The white throat is spotted pink, red or purple. Foxgloves are highly toxic, the drug digitalin – once widely used to treat heart complaints – being an extract of the leaves. The name foxglove is believed to derive from the likeness of the flower to an early musical instrument consisting of a string of varying size bells.
Similar species: None.

▶ LOUSEWORT
Pedicularis sylvatica
Family Scrophulariaceae

Flowering period: April to July.
Distribution: Very common component of more acid moors, marshes and damp heaths in both the NYM, Pennines and the Dales. Absent everywhere else due to lack of habitat.

This native biennial member of the figworts is semi-parasitic on the roots of grasses, where it is often seen growing alongside milkwort. The name refers to the lice often endemic to the places where the plant grows. It reaches heights of no more than 20cm and is normally many branched with

TOP LEFT: LOUSEWORT. RIGHT AND INSET: FOXGLOVE. BELOW: RAGGED ROBIN.

pinnate leaves having many pairs of feathery-looking toothed leaflets.

The two-lipped flowers are reddish-pink (rarely white), the upper lip the longest and almost hood-like, and sepals joined into a hairy or hairless calyx that is green with purplish veins. Some botanists consider the hairless or hairy to be two separate ssp., the latter being designated *P. hibernica*.

Similar species: MARSH LOUSEWORT (*P. palustris*) shares a similar habitat but is less common. It is also known as red rattle because of the way the dry seeds rattle in the capsule. This annual or biennial differs by having a single branched stem, often purplish, growing up to 50cm. Leaves are 20–40mm with many pairs of leaflets alternately arrayed on robust stems. The flowers are reddish or purplish-pink and have lips of equal length and a downy sepal tube, rather than hairless in the case of *P. sylvatica*. It flowers May to September.

❭ HONESTY
Lunaria annua
Family Cruciferae

Flowering period: April into May.
Distribution: A garden plant introduction from southeastern Europe and western Asia that has become naturalized throughout the county, along streams, roadsides and waste places.

This colourful member of the cabbage family is a biennial growing to heights of one metre, with stiffly hairy branching stems. The upper leaves are unstalked, pointed, oval or lanceolate and coarsely toothed. The scentless flowers, 25–30mm diameter, are four-petalled, dark pink or mauve, sometimes white, with the lobes veined with darker purple.

The fruit pods are practically circular, green at the outset, but during the ripening process become translucent and persist through the winter. The

pods are sometimes known as 'silver penny' and are popular in dried flower arrangements. The plant contains up to 40 per cent oil, the properties of which make the plant a potentially useful as a source of bio-lubricants, and also for combating multiple sclerosis.
Similar species: see DAME'S VIOLET (*Hesperis matronalis*).

❭ WATER AVENS
Geum rivale
Family Rosaceae

Flowering period: April to September.
Distribution: Common and widespread perennial in the western Dales but less so further east. In the NYM tends to be concentrated in the southwest and northeast, with a scattering elsewhere. Prefers calcareous soils.

Also known as Billy's button in some areas, this member of the rose family forms large colonies on riverbanks, wet shady grasslands, damp meadows, ditches, hedgebanks and woodland fringes. It is of medium height (up to 80cm), downy, and has basal leaves that are pinnate, while those higher up the occasionally branching stems become trefoil. The roots smell like cloves and have traditionally been used as a wine and ale flavouring.

The flowers are solitary, nodding on long purple stalks, and are bell-shaped formed from the generally dull purple sepals and orange-pink petals, sometimes tinged with yellow. Sepals are triangular pointed. Flowers are up to 15mm in diameter and length and the seedheads burr-like.
Similar species: Much more scarce is *G. intermedium*, a hybrid between *G. rivale* and *G. urbanum*. It reaches a similar height usually on the edge of woods. This is a much prettier flower with yellow petals and sepals of pale purple tinged green. Flowers from mid-spring until early autumn.

TOP: WATER AVENS (INSET: *G. x INTERMEDIUM* HYBRID). BELOW: HONESTY.

▶ GREATER PERIWINKLE
Vinca major
Family Apocynaceae

Flowering period: February to May.
Distribution: A scarce native perennial evergreen undershrub found as a naturalized garden escape in slightly shady habitats along roadsides and hedgerows near habitation. Quite rare in the west and in the NYM area.

This more or less prostrate plant has hairless stems to 60cm that root at the tip to form new plants. The shiny, rather fleshy, long-stalked leaves, 30–50mm long, are pointed lanceolate, untoothed and arranged in opposite pairs. Stipules are absent.
    The hermaphrodite flowers, 4–50mm across, are blue and solitary, with five spreading petals, barely notched and joined at the base to form a corolla surrounded by a ring of narrow, fringed sepals. Five stamens are joined to the petal tube, while the stigma forms a broad head. There are no bracts.
Similar species: LESSER PERIWINKLE (*V. minor*) is a less robust plant with narrower leaves and smaller (25–30mm diameter) flowers. It shares a similar habitat and is just as scarce as *V. major*.

▶ BUGLE
Ajuga reptans
Family Labiatae

Flowering period: April to June.
Distribution: Widely encountered addition to the plant communities of grassland, woodland and shady places on damp ground.

This short (30cm) perennial propagates by sending out creeping, rooting stems. The square stems are hairy on two sides and rise from a tuft of hairless leaves that are oblong and slightly-toothed. Leaves (20–75mm) are sometimes bronzy in appearance, the lowest long-stalked.
    The flowers are hermaphrodite, sky blue, sometimes but rarely white or pink, forming a leafy, sometimes purply spike of five or six whorls. Flowers are 12–16mm across and have dark (blackish-purple) bracts with five pointed sepals forming a calyx. Petals number five and form a tube with three obvious lower lobes and protruding stamens and one, branching stigma.
Similar species: Sometimes confused with self-heal (*Prunella vulgaris*).

▶ CHICORY
Cichorium intybus
Family Compositae

Flowering period: June to September.
Distribution: Very rare native perennial infrequently found along field margins and roadside verges or waste places. Extremely scarce in the Dales. Has been recorded from South Yorkshire and is making a slow comeback into the NYM.

The plant grows to a height of 30–120cm, with grooved stems having 300mm-leaves that are spear-shaped, pinnately lobed and short-stalked, the upper ones undivided, unstalked and clasping the stem. Leaves grow from the base, or are spirally arranged up the stem and lacking stipules. The swollen roots of this particular species were dried and ground to yield chicory.
    The short-stalked, bright chalk blue composite flowers, 25–40mm diameter, on well-branched, stiffly hairy stems, have two rows of bracts beneath them. Sepals are scale-like and outer florets strap-like. There are five stamens joined into a tube, and a two-lobed stigma on a long style.
Similar species: BLUE SOW-THISTLE (*Cicerbita macrophylla*) is just as rare – a garden escape that shares similar habitats between July and September. It grows to about 60cm and has flowerheads of a darker blue and 30mm in diameter.

▶ CORNFLOWER
Centaurea cyanus
Family Compositae

Flowering period: June to August.
Distribution: A scarce casual found occasionally on waste ground or roadsides. Favours sandy, acidic sub-soils. Absent from the Dales, rare in the NYM, and infrequent on the magnesian limestone belt, the Wolds and along the Holderness coast.

Also known as bluebottle, this downy, often much branching, native annual grows up to 90cm, has alternate grey-green leaves, the lowermost (10–20cm in length) pinnately lobed and stalked, the upper ones unstalked and lanceolate. The solitary flowers (15–30mm across) are hermaphrodite and have compound heads composed of many smaller flowers that are an intense blue on the periphery with smaller, purplish ones nearer the centre. These have flairing, tubular petals. The calyx is

TOP LEFT: CORNFLOWER. TOP RIGHT: BUGLE. CENTRE: GREATER PERIWINKLE. BELOW: CHICORY.

covered with overlapping black-tipped bracts that are brown and scaly with toothed margins.
Similar species: See PERENNIAL CORNFLOWER (*C. montana*)

▶ PERENNIAL CORNFLOWER
Centaurea montana
Family Compositae

Flowering period: May to August.
Distribution: This relation of the daisy is an infrequent garden escape that has colonized a few roadsides, grassy bankings and waste ground.

This mat-forming, creeping perennial grows to heights of 60cm and bears spectacular blue upright flower heads on downy stems. The leaves are unstalked lanceolate and arranged in opposing pairs, while the flowers are solitary, and can be up to 80mm across with scale-like, black-edged bracts. The rayed petals are deeply divided into three or four linear filaments. The plant is very popular with bees.
Similar species: See CORNFLOWER (*C. cyanus*).

▶ BLUEBELL
Hyacinthoides non-scripta
Family Liliaceae

Flowering period: April to June.
Distribution: Widely distributed plant of deciduous woodlands, particularly birch and oak, and hedge bottoms. It exists, but less abundantly, on upland limestone that was once wooded.

Also known as the wild hyacinth, this attractive and delicate member of the lily family often carpets woodland creating an ethereal blue 'haze' and pleasant bouquet. It is a bulbous perennial growing to a height of 50cm from a tuft of narrow hairless and toothless leaves.
    The fragrant flowers are hermaphrodite and azure blue, less commonly white, carried in a nodding, one-sided spike on hollow leafless stems. Individual blooms are 15–20mm, and bell-shaped with six spreading segments to the perianth, cream-coloured anthers, six stamens and one stigma.
Similar species: The GARDEN BLUEBELL (*H. non-scripta x hispanica [H. massartiana]*) is a hybrid with broader leaves and larger flowers. It frequents woods, hedgebanks and roadsides, often in close proximity with the native plant, to which it is a serious threat.

▶ GERMANDER SPEEDWELL
Veronica chamaedrys
Family Scrophulariaceae

Flowering period: April to June.
Distribution: An extremely commonplace plant throughout the NYM, the Dales and on the magnesian limestones east into the VoY, notably at Skipwith Common.

The name germander is a corruption of the Greek chamaedrys meaning ground oak, an allusion to the supposed similarity of the leaves to those of the tree. This native perennial of grasslands is one of the more striking of the speedwells and can grow to a height of 35cm. It is a sprawling plant bearing paired leaves on a hairy stem. The latter is distinguished by two opposite lines of hairs. The leaves are short or non-stalked, pointed oval with deep serrations.
    Flowers, 10–20mm, are bright blue with a lighter-coloured eye, usually white, in opposite stalked spiked clusters originating from the base of the upper leaves. Sepals are spear-shaped and 4–6mm long and hairy. Flowers have four petals of 4–6mm, joined at the base, with the lowermost being the smallest. There are two protruding stamens and one stigma with a swollen tip.
Similar species: GREY FIELD SPEEDWELL (*V. polita*) is considerably rarer, has similar leaves but smaller flowers without the paler eye. Flowers March to November.

▶ COMMON FIELD SPEEDWELL
Veronica persica
Family Scrophulariaceae

Flowering period: All year.
Distribution: This plant was introduced from Asia two centuries ago. Today it is a scarce arable weed in the east of our county, rare in the Dales.

This low sprawling hairy annual has branching stems reaching to 40cm with oval, coarsely-toothed leaves that are short-stalked, paired on the lower stem and alternate higher up. Flowers are sky blue with a paler blue or white lower petal, all delicately veined in darker blue. The flowers grow solitary from the leaf base and are hermaphrodite, 8–12mm across, with four unequal, oval sepals (4.5–7mm), two protruding stamens and one stigma with a bulbous tip.
Similar species: GREEN FIELD SPEEDWELL

TOP AND INSET: BLUEBELL. CENTRE LEFT: GERMANDER SPEEDWELL. RIGHT: PERENNIAL CORNFLOWER.
BELOW: COMMON FIELD SPEEDWELL.

(V. *agrestis*) is an equally rare plant with smaller, pale-coloured flowers (4–8mm) on shorter stems. Flowers from March to November.

SLENDER SPEEDWELL (*V. filiformis*) is sometimes called creeping speedwell. It is widely established as a mat-forming perennial in short grassland from April to June. It has leaves that are more round and flowers that are more mauve than blue and carried on long slender stalks.

▶ THYME-LEAVED SPEEDWELL
Veronica serpyllifolia
Family Scrophulariaceae

Flowering period: April to October.
Distribution: A very common creeping native perennial found throughout as a garden invader, on short grass, pathways, bare ground, forest rides and damp pastures. Favours acid soils.

Growing to 25cm, this creeping and rooting plant has stems that turn upwards and terminate in leafy, loosely flowering spikes. It lacks the toothed and hairy look of most species of Veronica, though a closer inspection reveals inconspicuous hairs and leaf serrations. Paired leaves are rounded oval, short-stalked and shiny. The tiny flowers (5–8mm across) are pale blue, sometimes white with purple or dark blue veins on the upper half. They have four petals and the bracts are longer than the flower stalks, which are longer than the calyx.
Similar species: HEATH SPEEDWELL (*V. officinalis*) is a species favouring stone walls, moor edges and dry grasslands on acid soils. It is particularly common in the NYM and the Dales. It has leaves that are more oval and more obviously toothed than in *V. serpyllifolia*. Flowers are lilac with darker veins and flower from May until October.

▶ WATER SPEEDWELL
Veronica anagallis-aquatica
Family Scrophulariaceae

Flowering period: June to August.
Distribution: An uncommon plant of water margins, marshy ground, ditches and dew ponds. This short (up to 25cm), creeping perennial has somewhat fleshy, unstalked and slightly-toothed, oval pointed leaves arranged in opposite pairs on hairless green stems. The pale blue flowers,

5–7mm diameter, grow in opposite pairs of spiked clusters on long stalks from the leaf axils.
Similar species: See BROOKLIME (*V. beccabunga*).

▶ BROOKLIME
Veronica beccabunga
Family Scrophulariaceae

Flowering period: May to September.
Distribution: An abundant and widespread inhabitant of clean shallow standing or slowly moving water – streams, ditches, marshes – or beside ponds, sometimes in wet meadows. Very common in both the Dales and the NYM. Also in the Wolds and elsewhere.

Sometimes known as water pimpernel, this robust creeping, hairless perennial likes having its feet wet. It has spreading roundish, sappy stems to 60cm carrying opposite pairs of fleshy leaves that are glossy, oval and slightly toothed. They have a rounded base and blunt tip. The leaf stalk is shorter than the blade. Stipules are absent.

The hermaphrodite flowers (10–30 in number) are 5–8mm across, deep blue and born in opposite, slender-stalked racemes originating from the axils of upper leaf pairs. The stalk is almost equal in length to the flower. There are four sepals each 2–4mm long, with joined bases and flat lobes; two protruding stamens, one stigma and one style. Brooklime once was used in combating scurvy.
Similar species: See WATER SPEEDWELL (*V. Anagallis-aquatica*).

▶ SPRING GENTIAN
Gentiana verna
Family Gentianaceae

Flowering period: May to June.
Distribution: Very rare. Grows in only one isolated mountain location in the northern Dales. This flower is listed as a seriously endangered species and is protected by law.

The pretty trumpet-shaped flower is a native low perennial and a true alpine species, growing on short stony turf on limestone. Reaching a height of only 5cm, this delightful plant forms a basal rosette of pointed, almost fleshy-looking, oval leaves, from which the short stem rises. Stem leaves are paired with no stipules.

Flowers, 15–20mm diameter, are solitary and upright with five rich blue pointed oval petals,

TOP LEFT: THYME-LEAVED SPEEDWELL. RIGHT: WATER SPEEDWELL. BELOW LEFT: SPRING GENTIAN. RIGHT: BROOKLIME.

6–8mm, forming a corolla up to 25mm in length. Sepals are narrow and pointed and a third the length of the petal tube, sometimes reddish-brown. Blooms sometimes refuse to open except on sunny days.

Similar species: MARSH GENTIAN (*G. pneumonanthe*) is equally rare and reduced to two wet heaths, one on a SSSI at the southwestern fringe of the Dales, the other in the VoY. It is a native perennial growing to heights up to 30cm, but usually much shorter. The leaves are linear, arranged in opposite pairs. The flowers have five petals forming a trumpet-shaped corolla, 25–40mm long, streaked on the outer surface with yellow or green. Flowers July to September.

▶ MEADOW CRANESBILL
Geranium pratense
Family Geraniaceae

Flowering period: June to September.
Distribution: An especially commonplace and pretty plant of rough grassy places, roadsides, hedgebanks and the like, on calcareous soils up to altitudes of 350 metres.

This medium (30–80cm) perennial is one of my all-time summer favourites. It sports splendid chalk blue or violet-blue hermaphrodite flowers 25–40mm across. These grow in stalked pairs from the leaf base and have five (15–20mm long) petals, not notched, with five (11–15mm long) bristle-tipped sepals, ten stamens and five slender stigmas. The bracts are triangular-shaped and narrow.

Leaves up to 150mm long grow from the base and on alternate sides of the hairy stem. They are palmate, deeply divided (almost to the base) into three to seven lobes and pointed at the tip. The lower leaves are long-stalked, the upper ones short or almost stalkless. Stipules are broad and papery.
Similar species: See WOOD CRANESBILL (*G. sylvaticum*).

▶ COMMON MILKWORT
Polygala vulgaris
Family Polygalaceae

Flowering period: May to early autumn.
Distribution: A common plant of all but the most acid grasslands in the Dales and NYM, also the Wolds, east coast and South Yorkshire.

This low to short (up to 30cm) trailing perennial has slender branching and upward-pointing stems, with 5–35mm long lanceolate leaves that are broader in their middle, or towards the base. The lowest leaves are broader than the upper ones. These are arranged alternately up the hairless or sparsely hairy stems and are stalkless. Stipules are absent.

Hermaphrodite flowers are 4–8mm usually white-tipped blue, though white, pink, mauve and purple variations are known. They form stalked spikes, of between ten and forty flowers. There are three fringed petals, eight stamens and a two-lobed stigma, five unequal sepals with large inner pair being brightly coloured. The name of the flower dates from a folklore belief that the plant was believed to aid the flow of milk in nursing mothers.
Similar species: HEATH MILKWORT (*P. serpyllifolia*) is very similar but more widespread. It has opposite leaves and ranges higher than its counterpart, even into the acid moorlands of the Pennines. Fairly common in the Dales and NYM, less so on the magnesian limestones. It has a similar flowering period.

DWARF MILKWORT (*P. Amarella*) is nationally very rare and only known from a handful of locations in the Dales. It differs from the other two species by having the lower leaves forming a rosette. Similar flowering period.

▶ HAREBELL
Campanula rotundifolia
Family Campanulaceae

Flowering period: July to September.
Distribution: Very abundant on dry grasslands everywhere, especially the valleys of the NYM. It is also a common sight on the limestone pastures of the Dales. Also present in the Wolds, the coastal fringe and South Yorkshire, but absent from the high moorlands with one exception, at Ogden Reservoir on the West Yorkshire moors.
Also known as the Scottish bluebell, this delicate native perennial grows to 40cm tall, has slender, slightly branched stems that are hairless and have roundish root leaves and linear stem leaves arranged alternately. Flowers are 15mm and five-petalled, forming a flaring bell on delicate stalks in loose nodding clusters. There are five slender sepals, five stamens and a single, three-lobed stigma.
Similar species: PEACH-LEAVED BELLFOWER (*C. persicifolia*) is an escapee from cultivation and

TOP: HAREBELL. BELOW LEFT: COMMON MILKWORT. RIGHT: MEADOW CRANESBILL.

a rare find along shady streams on the magnesian limestone. It is a medium-tall hairless plant with lower leaves stalked and oblong, the upper stem leaves unstalked and lanceolate. Flowers are much larger (up to 25mm) and in a stalked spike appearing from May to August.

❯ FIELD FORGET-ME-NOT
Myosotis arvensis
Family Boraginaceae

Flowering period: April to October.
Distribution: An extremely common plant throughout the county from a range of habitats, including cultivated ground, and bare and grassy places with not-too-acid soils.

Also called common forget-me-not, this softly hairy native annual or biennial has upright branching stems growing to 60cm but more usually half that height. The blunt oblong or lanceolate, slightly greyish-looking leaves (6–80mm long), are untoothed and short-stalked forming a basal rosette. Stem leaves are unstalked and arranged alternately with no stipules.
 The hermaphrodite flower heads are 3–5mm diameter, opening from pink buds into chalk blue or grey-blue flowers with a yellow eye. There are five oval and slightly pointed petals forming a flat head, with several flowers at tip of stem. Petals are 1.5–3mm long with five sepals, 2.5–7mm joined at the base, the calyx covered in hooked hairs. Bracts are absent. There are five stamens and one stigma.
Similar species: CHANGING FORGET-ME-NOT (*M. discolor*) is a much scarcer annual preferring open and sandy habitats, old quarries and walls, though sometimes found in damper situations. It has smaller (2mm) flowers. The plant is so-named because the flowers start out cream or pale yellow before changing to blue. The stem, rising from a basal rosette with lanceolate stem leaves arranged alternately, has spreading hairs in the lower half and depressed ones higher up. The calyx is covered with hooked hairs. Flowers May to June.

❯ WATER FORGET-ME-NOT
Myosotis scorpioides
Family Boraginaceae

Flowering period: June to September.
Distribution: A marginal species common everywhere beside ponds and slow-moving fresh water, also in marshes.

This creeping perennial is one of the prettier forget-me-nots. The stems and calyx are distinguished by being covered in closely pressed hairs. The lanceolate leaves are 20–50mm long, and are untoothed and unstalked, growing alternately up the stem. Flowers, 4–10mm diameter, have five sky blue (less commonly white or pink) only slightly notched petals with a yellow eye. Sepals are broad with short teeth and are conjoined for at least one third of their length.
Similar species: CREEPING FORGET-ME-NOT (*M. secunda*) is a nationally scarce plant, a component of acidic marshland and stream sides. It is more common in the Dales than anywhere else in the county. Lower stems have spreading hairs and flowers 4–8mm diameter that may be almost white, with sepal teeth cut to at least halfway. Flowers June to September.

❯ VIPER'S BUGLOSS
Echium vulgare
Family Boraginaceae

Flowering period: May to September.
Distribution: Nowhere can this calcicole species be regarded as common. Occasionally found in mostly dry situations: disused quarries, disturbed and waste ground in the Dales and similar habitats in the NYM. It is also recorded from RNR in West Yorkshire and along riverbanks in the VoY.

This is an attractively erect perennial. It has rough stem hairs to the point of being almost prickly, rising to heights of 100cm or so from a rosette of hairy, strap-like leaves. The latter are 100mm linear lanceolate and slightly wavy, the lowest broad and stalked, the upper ones unstalked and narrowing. The flowers (2cm long, 10–12cm broad) start off pink but turn a vivid purply-blue, sometimes flecked with pink. Blooms occur (thirty to forty in number) on branching spikes, and have five petals forming a flaring corolla with obvious red stamens protruding from the mouth. The plant gains its name from the belief in its powers over poisonous snakebites and toxic herbs. The name bugloss is from the Greek meaning ox's tongue.
Similar species: None.

TOP LEFT: FIELD FORGET-ME-NOT. RIGHT: WATER FORGET-ME-NOT. BELOW: VIPER'S BUGLOSS.

▶ GREEN ALKANET
Pentaglottis sempervirens
Family Boraginaceae

Flowering period: March to July.
Distribution: A medieval introduction to Britain's gardens, naturalized in damp and shady roadside situations, field margins and walls close to habitation. Nowhere is it common, though concentrations occurring near Whitby Abbey may suggest use by monks for medicinal purposes.

A medium-height (growing to 100cm) roughly hairy perennial with branching stems rising from a basal rosette. Leaves (30–400mm) are pointed and oval, the stem leaves, on alternate sides of the stem, and the lowest ones stalked. The leaf margins are usually wavy and stipules absent.

   Flowers (8–10mm across) are hermaphrodite and appear in long-stalked leafy groups of five to eight growing from the leaf axils. They are bright blue with a white centre and have five un-notched petals (6–8mm) joined at the base. There are five, narrowly spear-shaped sepals with blunt teeth, one club-shaped stigma and five stamens.
Similar species: None.

▶ BORAGE
Borago officinalis
Family Boraginaceae

Flowering period: May to September.
Distribution: A former garden herb once widely cultivated as a salad vegetable. It occurs in scattered localities in the NYM, the Wolds and on the magnesian limestones. Rare in the Dales.

A medium height, roughly hairy annual, the juice of which, some think, smells of cucumber. Growing to heights of 50cm the stems carry oval pointed leaves with wavy margins, the lowermost being stalked. An infusion from the leaves was reputed to aid recovery from a hangover. The five-petalled flowers are an intense sky blue, 20–25mm in diameter, hanging in nodding, loose clusters. They have narrowing, pointed petals and hairy green sepals, together with a prominent column of purply-black stamens extending beyond the corona.
Similar species: The extremely rare ABRAHAM, ISAAC & JACOB (*Trachystemon orientalis*) is known from just one or two sites in the Dales and NYM. This curiously named plant has larger leaves that are heart-shaped, mainly from the roots. It does not grow as tall as *B. officinalis* and carries leafless clusters of smaller, 15mm diameter, flowers that are purple with petal lobes folded down.

▶ SIBERIAN IRIS
Iris sibirica
Family Iridaceae

Flowering period: June to July.
Distribution: Uncommon. A garden escape found naturalized on roadsides close to habitation in a handful of scattered locations.

This is a tall (60–90cm) and spectacular plant preferring neutral to acid soils. A single stem has narrow, bright green grass-like leaves, and carries one to three elegant blooms at its tip. The 60mm flower has vivid blue-purple flared outer petals (falls), yellowing towards the base, three purple inner members (standards) and three erect petal-like purple stigmas that branch at their tips (crests). Because this is a garden escape there are other colour variations, including pure white and yellow.
Similar species: None.

▶ SEA HOLLY
Eryngium maritimum
Family Ubelliferae

Flowering period: June to September.
Distribution: Scarce; only near Spurn Point.

This very attractive cactus-like perennial is one of the more unusual of the carrot family. Favouring shingle and sandy habitats, the hairless stems grow to heights of 60cm. Leaves are basal or alternately arranged, and are leathery and blue-green with a waxy feel. They have vicious spiny margins and whitish veins, the uppermost leaves clasping the stem. Stipules are absent.

   Flowers (6–8mm) are hermaphrodite and grey-blue, growing in a thistle-like tightly-packed umbel (15–30mm long) with broad and spiny, leaf-like bracts. There are five petals (3–4mm long) that are narrow and notched, five sepals (4–5mm long), five inward-curving stamens and two slender stigmas.
Similar species: None.

TOP LEFT: GREEN ALKANET. RIGHT: SIBERIAN IBIS. BELOW LEFT: BORAGE. RIGHT: SEA HOLLY.

▶ YELLOW ARCHANGEL
Lamiastrum galeobdolon
Family Labiatae

Flowering period: May to June.
Distribution: An uncommon plant of old and well-established woodland, sometimes shady hedgebanks. Very rare in the Dales and scattered toward the east, on the magnesian limestones around Fountains Abbey, and in the Harrogate district. In the NYM there are good colonies in Kirkdale and in the valley of the lower Esk.

Sometimes called yellow dead-nettle, this relative of the mint is a patch-forming native perennial preferring medium acid soils. It grows up to 50cm in height, and is hairy with broad to lanceolate, nettle-like irregularly toothed leaves that are dark green, stalked and give off an unpleasant smell if crushed. The flowers grow in attractive whorls from the leaf axils of the upper leaves and are pale yellow, and as with other dead-nettles has upper petals forming a hood. The lower lobes are streaked with red or reddish-brown.
Similar species: LARGE-FLOWERED HEMP-NETTLE (*Galeopsis speciosa*) is very rare in the Dales, and only known from a handful of sites elsewhere. This native annual is a casual of waysides and open ground. It is taller (up to 80cm) than *L. galeobdolon*, roughly hairy, and has pale yellow flowers with lower lobe purple or purple-streaked. Flowers in whorls at base of upper leaves, appear from July to September.

▶ WALL FLOWER
Cheiranthus cheiri
Family Cruciferae

Flowering period: May to June.
Distribution: Very uncommon. A garden escape occurring in some localities, on walls, close to habitation. Extremely rare from the Dales. There are long-established colonies on the walls of Fountains Abbey and others to be seen at Staithes and Danby castle.

This is one of a group of species that are characteristic of ancient mortared walls. Growing up to 60cm tall, this attractive perennial member of the cabbage family is often semi-prostrate on somewhat woody stems bearing alternate, narrow lanceolate leaves that are untoothed and covered in flattened hairs. The fragrant flowers (up to 25mm diameter) have four widely-spaced petals presenting an obvious cross. They can be yellow, yellow-red or yellowy-brown in colour, streaked with red, and growing in crowded spikes.
Similar species: None.

▶ CHARLOCK
Sinapis arvensis
Family Cruciferae

Flowering period: April through to autumn.
Distribution: A weed of cultivation fairly commonplace in field margins and disturbed ground on calcareous soils. Abundant in the NYM and on the magnesian limestone corridor, but rare everywhere else.

This tall (30–80cm) member of the cabbage family is a roughly hairy annual with stems that are upright and branching with stiff hairs, though often glabrous higher up. The lowest leaves are large, 200mm, and irregularly-lobed and toothed. The upper leaves are arrow-shaped and pointed at the tip. Only the lowermost leaves are stalked.

Flowers, 12–18mm, are hermaphrodite and bright yellow with four spreading petals of 9–12mm. These form an elongated inflorescence containing numerous blooms. Sepals (four off) are spreading, with six stamens and a single two-lobed stigma. Bracts and stipules are absent. The fruits are pod-like, 25–40mm long, with a long beak-like tip.
Similar species: RAPE (*Brassica napus ssp. oleifera*) gives us the lurid yellow patches dominating arable landscapes. Introduced as animal fodder and for vegetable oil production, and now established as a casual on roadsides and waste ground. Rare in the Dales and NYM. Grows to 60cm and has greyish leaves, the uppermost stalkless and clasping, the lower ones pinnately lobed. Flowers are four-petalled bright yellow in a less elongated spike. Flowers April to August.

Wild turnip (*Brassica rapa*) is very rare in the Dales. Growing to 80cm, this annual is an arable escapee found as a casual along the coastal fringe of NYM. It is a roughly hairy plant, the lowest leaves pinnately lobed and upper ones arrow-shaped, stalkless and clasping. Flowers, 20mm, are white, occasionally yellow, four-petalled and form a flat-topped inflorescence appearing April to August.

TOP LEFT: YELLOW ARCHANGEL. RIGHT: WALL FLOWER. BELOW: CHARLOCK.

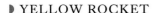

▶ YELLOW ROCKET
Barbarea vulgaris
Family Cruciferae

Flowering period: May to August.
Distribution: Common on the magnesian limestones, but less so in the Dales, and to the east. In the NYM it is very scattered.

A plant of damp field margins, hedgerows, waste places and riverbanks. Better known as common wintercress, this medium-tall hairless perennial grows to heights of 80cm and in common with other members of the crucifer family carries pinnately lobed, shiny dark green leaves. The upper ones are undivided, the lowest having two to five lobes more or less untoothed, the terminal lobe being the larger. The hermaphrodite flowers, 7–10mm, have four un-notched bright yellow petals and form many branched clusters at the top of the plant. These are dense at the outset but as the plant grows they become more lax.
Similar species: CREEPING YELLOWCRESS (*Rorippa sylvestris*) is quite rare in the north, though fairly frequent along some Dales riverbanks. Absent from NYM and scattered on the magnesian limestones. It is a straggling perennial with hairless stems of 45cm having deeply divided pinnate leaves, the lobes being spear-shaped and toothed, the uppermost not lobed. Is without the large end lobe of *B. vulgaris*. Flowers are 5mm with four yellow petals that are longer than the sepals. Flowers June to September.

▶ OPPOSITE-LEAVED GOLDEN SAXIFRAGE
Chrysosplenium oppositifolium
Family Saxifragaceae

Flowering period: March to July.
Distribution: The most common saxifrage, especially in the NYM, the Dales and, to a lesser extent, on the magnesian limestones. Also reported from West Yorkshire.

Not one of the most obvious, or pretty saxifrages, this low creeping, native perennial favours limestone flushes, marshland, the banks of shallow streams and stones therein, as well as damp shady places beneath bankings or boulders and in shady sinkholes. Given such habitats it is quite widespread in the Craven area.
    The squarish, slightly hairy stems carry roundish, bluntly toothed, almost fleshy leaves in opposite pairs. Root leaves are long-stalked. Flowers are inconspicuous (3–4mm) forming flattish yellowy-green heads without petals. There are four to five oval or triangular sepals and eight stamens. The anthers are bright yellow and the reason for the plant's name.
Similar species: Far less widespread is *C. alternifolium* (ALTERNATE-LEAVED GOLDEN SAXIFRAGE). This has a triangular section stem with alternate leaves that are broader and more deeply toothed. Flowers are slightly larger (5–6mm). Favours an identical habitat and flowering period.

▶ YELLOW MOUNTAIN SAXIFRAGE
Saxifraga aizoides
Family Saxifragaceae

Flowering period: June to August.
Distribution: Very rare (Yorkshire is the southern limit of this plant's range in Britain). Growing in only a handful of sites, most of them in the Three Peaks area between 200 and 400 metres altitude.

Found in base-rich flushes and beside springs, often trailing on rocks and scars. This mat-forming, slightly hirsute perennial grows to 20cm and has reddish-brown stems carrying alternately arranged, slightly toothed leaves clustered around the stem base. Leaves are spear-shaped and often reddening, giving a succulent appearance to the plant – one of the prettier of the family.
    The flowers (up to 18mm diameter) grow in lax heads. They have five oval petals that are yellow lightly blotched with red. Petals are well-spaced with prominent sepals almost equalling the petals in length but more pointed. There are three stigmas and ten stamens with obvious bright red anthers.
Similar species: See YELLOW PIMPERNEL (*Lysimachia nemorum*).

▶ YELLOW-WORT
Blackstonia perfoliata
Family Gentianaceae

Flowering period: June to November.
Distribution: Uncommon. This is the northern limit of its range for Britain. Absent from the Dales but scattered on the magnesian limestone. Also known from the coastal fringe, Wolds and Spurn

TOP: OPPOSITE-LEAVED GOLDEN SAXIFRAGE. BELOW LEFT: YELLOW ROCKET. RIGHT: YELLOW MOUNTAIN SAXIFRAGE.
BELOW: YELLOW-WORT.

Point. Recorded from Nether Poppleton, Askham Bog near York, the SFNR in South Yorkshire, and Kippax east of Leeds.

This perennial's preferred habitat is calcareous grassland. It is a pretty flower related to the gentians, and grows to heights of 50cm. The stems issue from a loose basal rosette and are bluish-green and hairless. The stem leaves are pointed oval and arranged in stalkless pairs joined at their base and clasping. This has the effect of appearing as if the stem is passing through the centre of a single leaf.

Flowers (12–18mm diameter) are bright yellow and variable, having between six and eight petals (4–8mm long) that are pointed oval and joined into a short tube at the base. The petals are longer than the sepals. Flowers appear in loosely branching clusters from base of the upper leaf pair and often close up if the sun is not shining.
Similar species: None.

▶ BOG ASPHODEL
Narthecium ossifragum
Family Liliaceae

Flowering period: July to September.
Distribution: A fairly common perennial. Locally abundant in parts of the Dales and NYM.

A plant of valley mires, bogs, flushes on peaty moors and sedge communities, sometimes growing alongside round-leaved sundew. Reaching 10–40cm tall, this is an attractive little plant on account of its yellow-orange starry flowers notable for their dense and attractive hairs on the stamen. The hairless stems, with few sword-like leaves up to 300mm long, terminate in an inflorescence from 25–100mm long consisting of 12–15mm flowers (six to twenty in number).

Flowers are hermaphrodite, with six pointed petals (6–8mm long), yellow to begin with but soon turning orange. There is one stigma and six orange, or red, filament-like stamens with bright orange or red anthers. This plant was once considered the culprit responsible for brittle bones in cattle, hence the Latin name ossifragum meaning 'bone breaker'. For such a stunning plant the flowers are brief, the heads turning a rich yellow after blooming.
Similar species: None.

▶ WILD TULIP
Tulipa sylvestris
Family Liliaceae

Flowering period: April.
Distribution: Known only from one site on the bank of the river Nidd near Cattal.

Growing to a height of 40cm, this hairless perennial was introduced to Britain and is more common in the southeast of the country. The grey-green leaves all grow from the base and are up to 25cm in length, grass-like with vague longitudinal veins, no ribs or grooves and are hooded at the tip.

The pretty, bright yellow flowers are pleasantly fragrant and 30–40mm across when fully opened. They grow solitary on a leafless stalk and resemble a slender garden tulip. There are eight stamens with orange anthers, and the base of the petals is occasionally tinged green or red.
Similar species: GARDEN TULIP (*T. gesneriana*) is found now and then along hedgerows, woodland fringes and roadsides close to habitation, where it will be a gardener's throw-out.

▶ KIDNEY VETCH
Anthyllis vulneraria
Family Leguminosae

Flowering period: April to September.
Distribution: An infrequent plant of well-drained calcareous grassland. Scattered in the Dales, on the magnesian limestones, in the VoY, all along the east coast, and a few inland locations in the NYM. Colonies tend to thrive on the boulder clay in sheltered sea coves and on cliffs.

Lady's fingers to some, this native perennial relative of the pea grows semi-prostrate to 60cm, and is silkily-hairy with alternate pinnate leaves up to 140mm. These are formed from lanceolate to oval leaves in five to fifteen short-stalked pairs. There are two leaf-like bracts at the base of each bloom.

Flowers are hermaphrodite forming compact heads on long stalks, sometimes paired. They are deep yellow, but can be orange, red, white or purple, or combinations of all colours. Five petals the lower pair joined, the uppermost the largest, while the side petals overlap. There are five unequal sepals forming an obviously woolly calyx. The seed pods are minute.

TOP: KIDNEY VETCH. BELOW LEFT: BOG ASPHODEL. RIGHT: WILD TULIP.

Similar species: HORSESHOE VETCH
(*Hippocrepis comosa*) is more scarce and absent
altogether from the NYM. Frequents well-grazed
turf on calcareous soils. Recorded from the
western Dales (though rare) and the Wolds. It is a
less robust plant with much more slender stems
and narrower, pinnate leaves ending in a leaflet.
Yellow flowers, five to twelve in number, comprise
less dense heads. Flowers from May to July.

▶ RIBBED MELILOT
Melilotus officinalis
Family Leguminosae

Flowering period: June to September.
Distribution: An introduction that is practically
absent from the Dales, scarcely more common on
the NYM, with only a peppering of sites in the
magnesian limestone belt and the Wolds.

Sometimes called common melilot (though
anything but), this tall (130cm) hairless biennial is
a plant of scrubland and waste places. The ribbed
stems bear trefoil leaves that are roundly toothed
and short-stalked. It forms a slightly bushy plant
with yellow flowers in crowded, stalked spikes.

Flowers have a keel shorter than wings. Six
sepals are joined in a calyx with prominent teeth,
the latter over half the length of the sepal tube.
Pods are hairless. As with all plants whose Latin
name ends with officinalis, this was regularly used
as a medicinal herb throughout the Middle Ages.
It was used in concoctions to treat swellings and
sore eyes.
Similar species: None.

▶ COMMON BIRDSFOOT TREFOIL
Lotus corniculatus
Family Leguminosae

Flowering period: May to September.
Distribution: A plant found practically throughout
the county. Absent, however from high moorlands
and arable areas.

This prostrate, cushion-forming, native perennial
is a component of short turf, roadsides and
grasslands. It obtains its name from the
resemblance of the seed pod to a bird's foot. This
sun-loving plant, also known as bacon and eggs,
has downy or hairless stems reach 10–40cm. The
latter have leaves consisting of two pairs of short-
stalked leaflets in opposition. These can be spear-

shaped or roundish, up to 20mm long, with a
single terminal leaf. The lowest pair of leaflets are
bent back so the leaf appears trifoliate.

The flowers (two to seven in number) are
hermaphrodite, yellow often tinged or streaked
with orange or red and 12–16mm long in long-
stalked heads. The 9–16mm long petals have
lowest pair joined, the uppermost the longest and
the lateral petals overlapping. Five sepals join to
form a toothed calyx. There is one stigma and ten
stamens joined at the base.
Similar species: GREATER BIRDSFOOT TREFOIL
(*L. pedunculatus*) is almost as abundant, but
prefers moors, marshes, drainage ditches and wet
grassland. It is larger with more erect hollow stems
and broader leaflets that are grey underneath. It
has five to twelve flowers in each head and
spreading sepal teeth. Flowers June to August.

▶ LESSER TREFOIL
Trifolium dubium
Family Leguminosae

Flowering period: May to September.
Distribution: A native annual common to the
Dales lowlands, the NYM and its valleys and on
the magnesian limestones.

Found on short turf and dry grasslands, also on the
fringe of paths and car parks. This is the smaller of
the three yellow-flowered, clover-like plants. It is
prostrate and almost hairless with trefoil leaves
having leaflets that are not pointed and slightly
toothed at the broader end of the lobe. The middle
leaflet is usually the longest-stalked. Flowers are
pale yellow, three to twenty in number, forming a
small clover-like head (8–10mm across), that
grows on a long slender stem. Seed pods are
straight and covered in dead flowers.
Similar species: HOP TREFOIL (*T. campestre*) is a
scarce annual of roadsides and short grassland,
growing to 30cm. It has twenty to thirty pale
yellow flowers in 10–15mm rounded clover-like
heads. The fruit resembles a small hop, hence the
name. Leaves are trefoil, the middle lobe long-
stalked and none of them having a terminal point.
Seed pods are curled like a butterfly's tongue.
Flowers May to September.

TOP LEFT: RIBBED MELILOT. RIGHT: COMMON BIRDSFOOT TREFOIL. BELOW: LESSER TREFOIL.

❯ BLACK MEDICK
Medicago lupulina
Family Leguminosae

Flowering period: April to August.
Distribution: A common component of short, lowland (not above 400 metres) grasslands and well-trodden pathways. Avoids ground that is too acid.

This slender, usually prostrate or sprawling, native annual often goes overlooked due to its flowers being so tiny. The branching, somewhat downy, stems grow to 80cm with trefoil leaves having 3–20mm long scarcely-toothed leaflets that are oval, or circular, sporting a minute terminal point. The tiny clover-like yellow, hermaphrodite flower heads form groups and consist of ten to fifty small pale florets, forming a dense but short-stalked head of 3–8mm. Seed pods are black and twisted.
Similar species: SPOTTED MEDICK (*M. arabica*) differs in being hairless or only slightly downy and usually has a dark spot on each leaflet. There are only one to four florets in each flower head.

❯ MEADOW VETCHLING
Lathyrus pratensis
Family Leguminosae

Flowering period: May to August.
Distribution: A commonplace lowland plant.

Found clambering over tall grasses, railway embankments, waste ground, hedges, scrub and forest margins. This native perennial, growing up to 1.2 metres, has robust angled stems that are hairless with obvious stipules at the base of the leaf stalks. Leaves are on opposite sides of stem and have a pair of lance-shaped leaflets, each pair with a tendril to aid climbing.

The hermaphrodite flowers are 4–12mm, vivid yellow and pea-like growing in loose clusters of five to twelve in number. Flowers comprise minute bracts, five sepals joined at the base with teeth equalling the tube in length. There are five greenish veined petals, 11–18mm long, with the uppermost the largest, the side pair overlapping the lower petal and the upper petal being the largest. There are ten stamens and one stigma, noticeably hairy on one side.
Similar species: None.

❯ LABURNUM
Laburnum anagyroides
Family Leguminosae

Flowering period: May to June.
Distribution: An introduced leguminous species that occasionally escapes from gardens and parks to become established in the wild. Sometimes found in light woodland, but often naturalized in ruderal situations.

Also known as the golden chain tree, this deciduous plant grows to 7 metres, often branching from its base. It has smooth bark and the seeds are very poisonous (never leave a pram-bound infant beneath it). Laburnum is a member of the pea family and therefore has trefoil leaves and the very distinctive keeled pea flower shape. These droop in lengthy racemes of paired brilliant yellow blooms very attractive to bees.
Similar species: None.

❯ GORSE
Ulex europaeus
Family Leguminosae

Flowering period: All year.
Distribution: Very common on low altitude acid soils everywhere, notably in waste places and scrubland. Far more common in the NYM, the coastal fringe and magnesian limestone belt than in the Dales.

Also known as furze, this much-branching native perennial evergreen grows to 2.5 metres and forms a distinctly straggly-looking spiny bush. Young plants have small trefoil leaves, but once mature it is liberally endowed with vicious 15–25mm long, furrowed spines, occasionally hairy at the base.
The pea-like flowers (12–18mm long) are short-stalked and grow in an inflorescence. They are an intense golden yellow with wings that are longer than the keel and yellowish sepals with spreading hairs as long as the petals. The blooms are richly scented of coconut and are prominent in late winter or early springtime.
Similar species: BROOM (*Cytisus scoparius*) is a deciduous shrub and early colonizer of roadsides, scrub and waste places in the lowlands. The grey-green hairless stems grow to 2 metres and are noticeably ridged. Unlike gorse they are spineless. The leaves are complex, being lanceolate and trefoil. The yellow flowers, 20–35mm, are winged

TOP LEFT: LABURNUM. RIGHT: BLACK MEDICK. BELOW LEFT: MEADOW VETCHLING. RIGHT: GORSE.

and keeled, the uppermost petal being the largest and sometimes streaked red or brown, the side pair sometimes spread outwards like wings. The prominent stamens are curved upwards with orange-brown anthers. Flowers grow in leafy stalked spikes from April to June.

DYER'S GREENWEED (*Genista tinctoria*) is much rarer, with a mere scattering of locations throughout the county. Also a spineless shrub but much shorter (to 60cm) than *C. scoparius*. It has smaller yellow flowers in leafy stalked spikes from June to August. Usual habitat is grassy places.

▶ COMMON PRIMROSE
Primula vulgaris
Family Primulaceae

Flowering period: March to May (occasionally into autumn and winter).
Distribution: This is one of the most commonplace and most easily recognizable flowers. Abundant on (but not solely) calcareous soils almost everywhere.

Commonly found in hedgebanks, open woodland, railway embankments, scrub and roadsides. The name comes from the Latin prima rosa ('first rose'). It is a low (to 20cm) perennial forming a leafy tuft. Individual leaves are 80–180mm in length, crinkly, notched and somewhat spoon-shaped or oval. These form an ideal base for the poses of lemon-coloured blooms. Stipules are absent.

The hermaphrodite flowers, 20–40mm, are darker toward the centre, and grow solitary on 50–200mm hairy stalks to form clusters of up to thirty blooms. Flowers have five shallowly notched petals (20–40mm) with five stamens and one stigma. Five sepals join into a calyx tube. *Similar species:* Forms hybrids with *P. veris* to produce FALSE OXLIP (*P. veris x vulgaris*), a less common plant in the Dales but found in scattered localities where both parents are present. The leaves gradually taper towards the base and flowers are a deeper yellow in umbels that are not one-sided as in the true oxlip.

▶ COWSLIP
Primula veris
Family Primulaceae

Flowering period: April to May.
Distribution: More of a calcicole species, this is not

quite so common as *P. vulgaris* due to it once having been a popular ingredient in wine-making.

This short, hairy perennial frequents open habitats beside roads, scrub and hedgebanks. It has crinkly leaves similar to those of *P. vulgaris* but abruptly narrowing towards the base and forming a rosette rather than a tuft. The leaves have small rounded teeth and are 50–200mm long.

The 10–15mm hermaphrodite flowers have five petals of a deeper yellow than the primrose, with orange spots in the centre. Petals form a flaring tube with five stamens and one stigma. Up to twenty-five blooms form a one-sided nodding cluster on a single stem, the latter anything up to 30cm tall, erect and leafless. *Similar species:* FALSE OXLIP (*P. veris x vulgaris*) is a much taller plant with darker yellow flowers not in one-sided umbels as with *P. veris*. The leaves taper more gradually towards the base.

▶ YELLOW PIMPERNEL
Lysimachia nemorum
Family Primulaceae

Flowering period: May to September.
Distribution: Very common throughout the NYM and the Dales, but less so further east and south of there. Scattered elsewhere. Known from the Hull area and Middleton Woods in West Yorkshire.

An abundant plant of hedgerows, ditches, stream sides, damp woodlands and forest rides on moist acid soils. This attractive little creeping perennial is a somewhat delicate plant, trailing hairless stems that reach 45cm with no stipules. The leaves (20–40mm long) are shiny green and carried on short stalks in opposing pairs. They are pointed oval and untoothed, the leaf stalk shorter than the blade.

The flat yellow flowers, 10–18mm diameter, are hermaphrodite and grow solitary on long stalks from the uppermost leaf axils. Five oval pointed petals, 6–8.5mm long, are joined at the base and wide-spreading. There are no bracts but five stamens, one stigma on a long style and five slender, pointed sepals of 3.5–6mm. *Similar species:* CREEPING JENNY (*L. nummularia*) is a less common plant found beside fresh water and in ditches. Much scarcer in the Dales and magnesian limestones and very rare in NYM. Recorded from drainage ditches in the VoY and a few places in the Wolds. It has rounded

TOP: COMMON PRIMROSE. BELOW LEFT: YELLOW PIMPERNEL. RIGHT: COWSLIP.

or heart-shaped leaves and larger (15–25mm) yellow, five petalled bell-like flowers that never fully open. The sepal teeth are broad. Flowers June to August.

❯ WELSH POPPY
Meconopsis cambrica
Family Papaveraceae

Flowering period: June to August.
Distribution: This species was originally confined solely to Wales and southwest England and is the only European representative of an essentially Himalayan and Chinese genus. It is a common garden escape that has established itself, often well-removed from habitation.

Unusually growing on walls, but more often hedgebanks, damp woods, roadsides or waste places. It is a slightly hairy, long-stalked plant, up to 50cm high, with deeply lobed root leaves and similar yet short-stalked leaves further up the stem. The papery flowers (50mm in diameter) have four, overlapping deep yellow petals.
Similar species: There is an orange-flowered variant.

❯ YELLOW RATTLE
Rhinanthus minor agg.
Family Scrophulariaceae

Flowering period: May to September.
Distribution: Known from a few scattered locations in West and South Yorkshire, the east coast and Spurn Point, but fairly commonplace in the NYM area and the Dales, less frequent on the magnesian limestones.

This native annual of sunny unimproved meadows, rough hill pastures and waysides is semi-parasitical on grasses and other meadow herbs, obtaining some of its nourishment through conjoined roots. It is perhaps known best when in fruit, when the seeds rattle within the capsule. Growing to heights of up to 40cm, this almost hairless plant has often black spotted stems, sometimes branched, that have opposite pairs of oblong or linear, stalkless toothed leaves (10–50mm long). Stipules are absent.
    The hermaphroditic flower forms a leafy spike, 12–15mm long, and is yellow or purply tinged on a stalk much shorter than the bloom with bracts that are leaf-like and triangular. Being a member of

the figworts it is a two-lipped flower with four sepals of 12–18mm joined into a broad, bulb-like calyx. The five petals are 12–15mm in length joined in a tube with the upper two forming a hood. There are four stamens underneath the upper petals, and one stigma.
Similar species: None.

❯ COMMON COW-WHEAT
Melampyrum pratense
Family Scrophulariaceae

Flowering period: May to September.
Distribution: Less common than yellow rattle, especially in the Dales where it is quite rarely seen. Absent from the magnesian limestone belt and an occasional find in the NYM area.

Preferring heaths, woodland and woodland rides, shady bankings and verges, this member of the figworts is a delicate but straggly-looking plant growing to heights up to 50cm. It is semi-parasitic on other woody species. Has slightly downy or occasionally hairless stems carrying pairs of untoothed, unstalked and shiny lanceolate leaves.
    The flowers (12–18mm long) are pale yellow, but sometimes tipped red, pinkish or pale purple, and has a slender calyx tube with long pointed sepal teeth, curved upwards. The two-lipped flowers have a closed mouth and grow in pairs facing the same direction from the base of toothed, leafy bracts. The upper lobes have lips that are fringed with fine hairs.
Similar species: None.

❯ YELLOW TOADFLAX
Linaria vulgaris
Family Scrophulariaceae

Flowering period: June to October.
Distribution: Not the common find it once was, although it was always more scarce in the North. Frequent on the magnesian limestone corridor, but less so in the Dales, the NYM and in the Wolds. Recorded from a few locations in West Yorkshire.
    A plant of waysides, verges and waste places. Sometimes referred to as common toadflax, this upright native perennial is a pretty species growing to heights of 30–80cm with hairless branching stems lacking stipules. The narrow, grey-green leaves (20–60mm long), are linear or spear-shaped and untoothed, growing spirally around the stem.

TOP LEFT: WELSH POPPY. RIGHT: YELLOW RATTLE. BELOW LEFT: COMMON COW-WHEAT. RIGHT: YELLOW TOADFLAX.

The hermaphrodite flowers, yellow with an orange spot on the lower lip, are snapdragon-like and grow, five to thirty in number, in a crowded spike. Five petals (20–33mm long) form a corolla with a slightly curving 15–30mm long spur at the base; with four stamens, paired, and one stigma carried on a slender style. The flower stalk is noticeably shorter than the flower. A calyx (3–6mm) is formed of five sepals with oval pointed teeth.
Similar species: None.

❭ GREAT MULLEIN
Verbascum thapsus
Family Scrophulariaceae

Flowering period: June to August.
Distribution: A fairly common plant but scarce in the Dales. Uncommon in the NYM, where it is usually found on dry grassy bankings but absent from acid and peaty soils.

A plant of waste ground on calcareous soils. This plant, also known as Aaron's rod, has to be a candidate for our most imposing wild flower. It is a native biennial growing much taller (up to 2 metres) than its cousin *B. nigrum*. Though usually poker straight the stem sometimes branches and, together with the leaves, is thickly covered in white woolly hair. Leaves are lanceolate, bluntly toothed and anything up to 400mm in length with winged stems. The first year's leaf growth forms a rosette, with later leaves spiralling up the robust stem.
Flowers are almost flat, some 12–30mm in diameter, hermaphrodite and yellow with five petals (6–14mm). Five pointed sepals (8–12mm) are joined at the base, the lobes pointed oval. There is one stigma and five stamens, three whitely hairy and two hairless. Flowers are numerous and form a much denser spike than *B. nigrum*. The plant once had many uses, the blooms used in cough medicine and the dried flower tops making tapers.
Similar species: See DARK MULLEIN (*B. nigrum*).

❭ DARK MULLEIN
Berbascum nigrum
Family Scrophulariaceae

Flowering period: June to September.
Distribution: Far less common than *V. thapsus* since it is at its northern limit for Britain.

Recorded in lower Eskdale, Glaisdale and a few scattered locations in the VoY.

A native biennial preferring disturbed ground or roadside grassy verges. It forms a handsome plant growing to 1.2 metres. The usually unbranched, hairy (but not woolly) stem is often purplish and carries heart-shaped toothed leaves that are dark green, hairy and stalked. These form a rosette from which the flowering stem rises. The hermaphrodite flowers (12mm diameter) form upright spikes and have five bright yellow petals with purple or red hairs on the stamens giving the flower the appearance of a darker centre.
Similar species: See GREAT MULLEIN (*V. thapsus*).

❭ MONKEY FLOWER
Mimulus guttatus x luteus [M. x robertsii]
Family Scrophulariaceae

Flowering period: June to September.
Distribution: Commonplace hybrid found throughout the Dales and NYM.

Often found in clumps alongside streams and on shingle banks in the major river valleys, also in drainage ditches and marshes. Almost succulent-looking, this prostrate creeping perennial grows to 20cm. It has hairless, reddish-looking stems carrying opposite pairs of oval pointed leaves with toothed wavy edges. The lowermost leaves are stalked, the upper unstalked and clasping the stem.
Flowers (25–30mm) are long-stalked and grow from the axils of the upper leaves. They have five bright yellow petals, the lowermost three lobes longer, red speckled and all joined at the base into a corolla. Five sepals (25–45mm) form an angled calyx. There are four stamens in pairs and one stigma.
Similar species: *M. guttatus* is rare in the North. Introduced from the Aleutian Islands in 1812. Found in only a handful of scattered riverside locations. It is a perennial creeping plant growing to around 20cm and is hairless beneath but stickily hairy in the flowerhead. The stems carry opposite pairs of slightly irregularly toothed, oval to roundish leaves (10–70mm), with the lowermost ones stalked, the upper not. Stipules are absent. Flowers, 25–45mm, grow at stem tips and are a golden yellow, two-lipped with an open 'throat' spotted with red. Flowers June to September.

TOP LEFT: GREAT MULLEIN. RIGHT: DARK MULLEIN. BELOW: MONKEY FLOWER.

▶ CARLINE THISTLE
Carlina vulgaris
Family Compositae

Flowering period: July to September.
Distribution: Not that common. Has a scattering on the magnesian limestone, in the NYM and the Wolds. Slightly more abundant in the Dales.

A plant of short grassland on calcareous soils, often on steep sunny slopes and in disused quarries. This unusual-looking biennial grows to heights of 60cm (but more usually no more than 30cm). The unbranched upright stem is often reddish and bears basal leaves as well as stalkless alternate, pinnately lobed bright green leaves, each lobe armed with a spine. The uppermost leaves broaden towards the base. Stipules are absent and what hairs are present are sparse and cotton-like.

Flowers (20–40mm diameter), are hermaphrodite and two to five in number at the top of the stem. The disk florets of the flowerheads are honey-coloured, sometimes purplish, and enclosed by strap-shaped outer ray floret-like bracts. The latter are yellowish or silvery, often turning upwards towards their tips in damp weather. Sepals form a ring of hairs; five stamens form a tube with one stigma divided into two lobes.
Similar species: None.

▶ GOLDEN-ROD
Solidago virgaurea
Family Compositae

Flowering period: June to September.
Distribution: Not all that commonplace. Can be found in the Dales, at a scattering of sites in the western fringe of the VoY and in the NYM.

A plant of undisturbed waste places, scrubland, roadsides, cliff faces, old quarries, woodland margins and rocky terrain. This medium (up to 75cm) height perennial may be short-haired or not, the scarcely branched stems bear bluntly oval or lanceolate leaves (20–100mm) arranged spirally around the stem. Leaves are toothed and short-stalked or not at all. Stipules are absent.

The hermaphrodite flowers (8–20mm in diameter) are yellow and daisy-like, rather similar to ragwort, with tiny florets surrounded by long clusters of bracts. Flowers are narrow and 4–8mm in length and yellowish green. Inner florets (ten to thirty in number) are 4–6mm tubular and the outer florets (female) from six to twelve in number and 6–9mm long and strap-shaped. There are five petals joined in a corona surrounded by a ring of hair-like sepals. There are five stamens and one stigma.
Similar species: None.

▶ CANADIAN GOLDEN-ROD
Solidago canadensis
Family Compositae

Flowering period: July to September.
Distribution: Quite scarce in the Dales and NYM, slightly more common on the magnesian limestone. Infrequent elsewhere.

A garden escape that has established itself in scattered locations, often on waste places, roadsides and railway embankments close to habitation. This unbranched, tall downy perennial has much more profuse, smaller yellow flowers than common golden-rod. They are held in a branching, one-sided slightly arching inflorescence. Flowers have very short ray florets. Leaves are lanceolate with three veins and prominently toothed towards the end third.
Similar species: None.

▶ SMOOTH SOW-THISTLE
Sonchus oleraceus
Family Compositae

Flowering period: March to November.
Distribution: Common throughout the county.

An abundant lowland weed found in pavement cracks, wall bottoms, waste ground and hedgerows. Growing up to 1.5 metres, this annual has hairless, angular hollow stems that weep a milk-like sap if cut. These have pointed oval or arrow-shaped lobed pinnate leaves with the end lobe being the largest and margins softly spined. Leaves can be greyish-green and are 60–250mm long, clasping the stem and arranged spirally.

Flowers are hermaphrodite, 20–25mm across, pale yellow growing in loose clusters. Individual flower heads are dandelion-like formed of tiny florets surrounded by rows of rays with bracts beneath. There are hair-like sepals; five stamens and one stigma making up the flowerhead. Like dandelions, the pappus makes a 'clock' of parachute seeds.

TOP: CARLINE THISTLE. BELOW LEFT: GOLDEN -ROD. RIGHT: CANADIAN GOLDEN-ROD. BELOW: SMOOTH SOW-THISTLE.

Similar species: The PRICKLY SOW-THISTLE
(*S. asper*) is equally as widespread sharing a similar
lowland habitat. Again it is an annual growing to a
height of 1.5 metres, the five-angled hollow stem
bearing less obviously lobed leaves that are
sometimes totally undivided with sharper-spined
margins. These are clasping and arranged spirally
on the stems.

Flowers have 20–25mm diameter heads with
florets enclosed by long smooth bracts. Florets are
10–15mm, flattened and yellow, sometimes purply
beneath. Sepals are hair-like as with *S. oleraceus*.
There are five stamens forming a tube, and a
two-lobed stigma on a long style. Similar
flowering period.

▶ WALL LETTUCE
Mycelis muralis
Family Compositae

Flowering period: July to September.
Distribution: Widespread in the NYM area and
Dales, less common on the magnesian limestones
and scarce anywhere else.

This native member of the daisy family is a
frequent plant of calcareous rocks, cliff faces,
disused quarry faces, limestone pavements grikes
and wall crevices. It is a hairless herbaceous
perennial growing to heights of 1 metre. The
delicate, branching stems often purple-tinged, bear
opposite pairs of dandelion-like clasping leaves.
These are pinnately lobed, dark green with a silky
sheen and slight reddish tinge, the terminal lobe
being the larger.

The smallish flowers (7–10mm across) are pale
yellow and occur in loose clusters carried on wiry,
multi-branched stems. They have only five ray
florets, divided into teeth at the ends. The leaves
are sometimes eaten as a complement to salads.
Similar species: NIPPLEWORT (*Lapsana
communis*) is a much more widespread, but usually
taller annual of wasteland and verges, riverbanks
and hedgerows. Never found in limestone
pavements. It can be distinguished from *Mycelis
muralis* by its hairy stems and multi-floret
(eight to fifteen in number) flowerheads which
are 15–20mm diameter.

Leaves (10–150mm long) have wavy teeth,
the lowermost dandelion-like. They are basal or
spirally arranged up the stem. Florets are strap-
like, pale yellow surrounded by eight to ten

hairless bracts. Sepals are hair-like. There are five
stamens joined in a tube and a single, two-lobed
stigma. Was formerly used as a salad plant.
Flowers July to September.

▶ GOATSBEARD
Tragopogon pratensis
Family Compositae

Flowering period: June to July.
Distribution: Much more common on the
magnesian limestones than the Dales, NYM or
anywhere else.

A frequent component of tall, lowland grass
communities, usually along roadsides, woodland
fringes, railway cuttings, embankments and
riversides. Also known as Jack-go-to-bed-at-noon
because of the way the flowers tend to open only
on sunny mornings and close again by mid-day.
Growing to 60cm this annual or perennial has
hairless stems, scarcely branching, with linear,
grass-like upright leaves of 100–300mm length.
These have whitish veins and grow from the base
or are spirally arranged around the stem.

The yellow flowers are solitary, and dandelion-
like. The best identifying feature is the sepal-like
bracts that are usually longer than the ray florets.
Flower heads are 15–22mm across and consist of
strap-like hermaphrodite florets (20–25mm long),
surrounded by bracts 25–30mm in length. The
sepals form a ring of hairs. There are five stamens
and a single two-lobed stigma. The plant becomes
more obvious when in seed, when the plant is
topped by an enormous pappus.
Similar species: None.

▶ COMMON FLEABANE
Pulicaria dysenterica
Family Compositae

Flowering period: July to September.
Distribution: Quite scarce in the Dales and on the
magnesian limestones, so too in the east except
where it is concentrated along the coastal fringes.

A plant of damp lowland habitats: beside ponds,
roadsides, streams, ditches and coastal cliffs where
it is abundant on the boulder clay. This medium
height perennial has 60cm branching stems that
are sparsely hairy with lanceolate leaves, 30–
80mm long, arranged spirally and clasping the
stem. Leaves are densely hairy beneath and have

TOP: WALL LETTUCE. BELOW LEFT: COMMON FLEABANE. RIGHT: GOATSBEARD.

wavy margins hardly toothed. Stipules are absent. Flowers are daisy-like some 15–30mm across, growing in loose, flat-topped upright clusters. The yellow florets are surrounded by many thin and hair-like bracts. The inner florets are hermaphrodite, 5–6mm long and tubular; the outer florets female, 8–11mm long and narrow. There are five stamens joined into a tube, and a single, two-lobed stigma. This plant was used in the past to repel fleas, hence the name, and floors were covered with it to serve such a purpose.
Similar species: ELECAMPANE (*Inula helenium*) is similar but much taller plant (over 60cm) and has larger flowerheads with broad bracts, and much broader, elliptical toothed leaves. Flowers are 60–80mm across, with narrow, yellow rays. This is a rare plant in our area, originally a garden plant cultivated for medicinal purposes, but now found in few places in the wild, usually roadsides. Flowers June to September.

▶ DANDELION
Taraxacum officinale
Family Compositae

Flowering period: April through to late summer.
Distribution: Probably the most ubiquitous and well-known (especially to irate gardeners) of plants, the dandelion scarcely needs any introduction. A component of waste ground, roadside verges, lawns and village greens.

This short perennial has a basal cluster of deeply lobed and variably toothed oval or spear-shaped leaves 50–400mm long. Stems are unbranched and hollow exuding a milky juice that turns the skin black. The flowers are solitary and 30–60mm across comprising many hermaphrodite 15–20mm long strap-like florets. The latter are yellowy-brown towards the centre. A ring of recurved sepal-like bracts occur beneath the florets. The seedhead pappus forms the 'clock' known to children everywhere.
   Dandelion has had many uses down the centuries. If collected and infused when they are fully open the flowers make an excellent wine. The leaves can be blanched and used in salads, while the roots, when dried, ground and roasted, make a coffee substitute, much used during the period of rationing imposed by the War. Dandelion tea is also said to be beneficial for kidney and liver problems.

Similar species: There are many ssp. that are difficult to differentiate, some confined to very specific locations.

▶ MOUSE-EAR HAWKWEED
Pilosella officinarum [Hieracium pilosella]
Family Compositae

Flowering period: May to October.
Distribution: A common component of well-drained unimproved grassy places, calcareous pastures, waysides, grazed heaths, old quarries and verges.

A short-medium height (to 25cm) creeping perennial with spoon-shaped leaves that are untoothed and whitish with dense hairs on the underneath, hairy above. The plant varies in hairiness, sometimes downy bordering on being shaggy in appearance. Leaves form a rosette rising from which a single stem carries the solitary flower. The stem is leafless though it can have a few scales.
   The pale yellow flowers (20–30mm diameter) have ray florets that are toothed at the end and are sometimes reddish striped or tinged on the under surface. Has the appearance of a dandelion but lacks the divided leaves. The plant was once used as a herbal treatment for Hepatitis.
Similar species: There are several ssp. some identified only from the Dales and West Yorkshire.

▶ TANSY
Tanacetum vulgare
Family Compositae

Flowering period: July to October.
Distribution: Quite a scarce lowland plant in the Dales and NYM, in the latter concentrated more towards the coast. Slightly more abundant on the magnesian limestone belt but infrequent anywhere else. Recorded from a few sites in South Yorkshire.

Usually seen on riverbanks, woodland fringes and roadsides. The name of this tall (up to 150cm) species comes from the Greek meaning 'immortality'. It is a native unbranched hermaphrodite plant that is almost hairless and aromatic. The robust, sometimes reddish stem bears deeply divided feathery-like pinnate leaves arranged spirally. Leaf stalks are short to absent with no stipules.
   Flowers are a rich yellow, rayless and button-

TOP: DANDELION. BELOW LEFT: TANSY. RIGHT: MOUSE-EAR HAWKWEED.

like (7–12mm), growing in flat-topped umbels. Bracts are paper-like and enclose the disc florets. Sepals form an inconspicuous rim. There are five stamens, joined to form a tube, and a two-lobed stigma. This plant is poisonous, but was formerly cultivated as a medicinal and culinary herb.
Similar species: None.

▶ COLTSFOOT
Tussilago farfara
Family Compositae

Flowering period: February to April.
Distribution: A real survivor this plant, and very commonplace throughout the county, especially on the boulder clays of the coast.

Found on heavy clay soils and along waysides, pavements, verges, waste ground and riverbanks. This short native perennial grows to 25cm, is one of the earliest plants of the season to appear, this being by virtue of the thick underground stems capable of storing nutrients. The unbranched, downy stem has purplish scales, with large stalked root leaves (100–300mm long) that are heart-shaped with pointed teeth, appearing long after the flowers.

Flowers (15–35mm) are solitary, yellow and dandelion-like with narrow ray florets enclosed by a single row of blunt bracts. The flowers are hermaphrodite, the few inner florets being male, the more numerous outer ones female. Sepals consist of a row of hairs. There are five stamens forming a tube, together with one stigma.
Similar species: None.

▶ RAGWORT
Senecio jacobaea
Family Compositae

Flowering period: June to November.
Distribution: A tenacious and common plant throughout.

This plant is an extremely widespread colonizer of pastures, as well as waste ground, railway embankments and other grassy places. A native biennial growing to 1.5 metres in height, this scarcely branched, hairless plant is quite poisonous to horses and cattle. The leaves, 25–200mm long, are either basal or arranged spirally up the stem; pinnately lobed with blunt-toothed lobes, the terminal lobe smallest.

The hermaphrodite flowers are deep yellow, 12–25mm diameter and daisy-like, carried in dense, flat-topped upright clusters. There outer (ray) florets (eleven to fifteen in number) are 6–12mm long, with five stamens and one stigma. Bracts are oblong and pointed, sepals merely a ring of hairs.
Similar species: MARSH RAGWORT (*S. aquaticus*) is much less common but easily distinguishable from *S. jacobaea* because it is a more widely branched plant with larger (25–30mm diameter) flowerheads and green bracts. The lower leaves are variable, from oval to pinnate. Favoured habitat is wet grassland and beside fresh water.

▶ OXFORD RAGWORT
Senecio squalidus agg.
Family Compositae

Flowering period: May to September.
Distribution: Introduced from Sicily in the late 1600s, this species is fairly widespread but quite scarce in the Dales. It is especially common around Whitby.

A common colonizer of building sites, waste ground, roadsides and railway embankments, it is a medium (30–100cm) height perennial, with reddish, well-branched and hairless stems. It is distinguished from *S. jacobaea* in having ragged, somewhat fleshy-looking, lanceolate to pinnately lobed leaves, the terminal lobe being sharp pointed. The uppermost leaves clasp the stem.

Flowerheads occur in flat-topped, open clusters, are 15–20mm diameter and usually have thirteen brilliant yellow outer ray florets encircling the densely-packed disk florets. They have black-tipped sepal-like bracts.
Similar species: None.

▶ GROUNDSEL
Senecio vulgaris
Family Compositae

Flowering period: All year round.
Distribution: Ubiquitous weed of disturbed ground, growing on soils of variable pH values.

The name of this plant is said to originate from the early Anglo-Saxon *grundeswelge*, meaning 'ground glutton'. It is a rather inconspicuous, often downy annual growing to heights of 45cm. The succulent

TOP LEFT: COLTSFOOT. RIGHT: RAGWORT. BELOW LEFT: OXFORD RAGWORT. RIGHT: GROUNDSEL.

stems bear spirally arranged leaves that are irregularly lobed pinnate. These are shiny green and hairless above, with stalks that are either short or absent. There are no stipules. Although the plant is poisonous to most mammals, the leaves are a favourite food source for rabbits.

Stems are slightly branching and carry loose clusters of hermaphrodite yellow flowers (4–5mm diameter) that grow upright cylindrical and brush-like, lacking ray florets. Flowerheads are unstalked at the outset, becoming stalked later. The disk florets (5–7mm long) are tubular and surrounded by a ring of sepal-like bracts that are noticeably black-tipped.
Similar species: STICKY GROUNDSEL (*S. viscosus*) is a much taller plant with a foetid smell and a greyish appearance with sticky hairs. The identifiable feature is the bracts which are not black-tipped as in *S. vulgaris*. The flowers are also a paler yellow with short, rolled-back rays. Flowers June to October.

▶ BITING STONECROP
Sedum acre
Family Crassulaceae

Flowering period: May to July.
Distribution: Widespread in the Dales, much less so on the magnesian limestone and everywhere else. Very common on limestone rocks and buildings.

A native perennial that thrives in the niches of walls, bridges, old barn roofs and rocky places in the sun. It seems especially to favour derelict buildings. Sometimes also called wall pepper because of its 'hot' taste, this creeping and mat-forming evergreen grows to 10cm with hairless stems bearing spirally arranged short-stalked leaves (3–5mm long) that are cylindrical, yellowish and succulent-like.

The bright yellow, star-like hermaphrodite flowers (12mm diameter) occur near the stem tip two to four to a branch in slightly branching heads. Flowers have five, spear-shaped petals (8–9mm long). There are five blunt-tipped oval sepals, ten stamens and five stigmas. Bracts are absent.
Similar species: REFLEXED STONECROP (*S. reflexum*) is much rarer, a garden escape colonizing waste ground close by habitation. It has short, erect flowering stems with longer (8–20mm) cylindrical leaves and six-petalled yellow starry

flower (15mm diameter), in tight flattish heads. Flowers June to August.

▶ YELLOW IRIS
Iris pseudacorus
Family Iridaceae

Flowering period: June to August.
Distribution: Common throughout in water meadows, marshes, drainage ditches, pond, canal fringes and riversides where it often forms attractive clumps.

This native perennial is also known colloquially as 'yellow flag', and grows to 1.5 metres with branched stems. The bluish-green leaves (120–900mm in length) are straight-sided, have parallel veins and a raised mid-rib. They are either basal or on the flowering stem. Hairs and stipules are absent.

The hermaphrodite flowers are 80–100mm across, growing one to three together. Petals are yellow with orange blotches or purple-spotted at the base. The perianth has six elements that are joined at the base: three broad, outer petals (50–75mm) that turn down at the edges, together with three upright inner ones (20–30mm). There are three stamens and three, petal-like broad stigmas. The paper-like bracts are 40–100mm long.
Similar species: None.

▶ YELLOW WATER-LILY
Nuphar lutea
Family Ranunculaceae

Flowering period: June to September.
Distribution: Recorded from a few sites in West Yorkshire, ponds in the VoY and the river Derwent. Known only from a couple of sites in the Dales, but slightly more common on the magnesian limestone belt.

This component of ponds and slow-moving freshwater is an aquatic native perennial known also by the name brandy bottle because of the shape of the flower bud. It has stout submerged stems bearing both submerged and floating leaves. The submerged ones are likened to those of cabbage; floating leaves are larger (40cm) than the white water-lily. These are heart-shaped or broadly oval, with a deep cleft, and are leathery in appearance, green, and long-stalked. In faster water the floating leaves may be absent.

TOP LEFT: YELLOW IRIS. RIGHT: BITING STONECROP. BELOW: YELLOW WATER LILY.

The hermaphrodite flowers are smaller (4–6cm in diameter) than those of the white water-lily, and often appear tightly-wrapped rather like a large globeflower. They always stand just clear of the water on long stalks. There are five prominent yellow sepals, 20–30mm, and numerous inconspicuous petals, many stamens and up to twenty stigmas.
Similar species: None.

▶ GLOBEFLOWER
Trollius europaeus
Family Ranunculaceae

Flowering period: May to August.
Distribution: Yorkshire is the southernmost limit of the range for this species in Britain. Two of the best places to see it are in the Dales, at Park Close and the Globeflower Reserve near Malham. It can also be found in Rydale in the NYM.

A not-too-commonplace upland plant of damp grassland, marshes, undisturbed woodland and also the humus-filled grikes of limestone pavements. This magnificent plant is a hairless perennial growing to 50cm with branching stems that have palmate leaves. Root leaves are cut to the base into five lobes, each in their turn divided into a further three lobes that are deeply toothed. Stem leaves are even more deeply cut into narrower segments.
   The vivid yellow flowers are 15–25mm diameter forming almost spherical tight buttercup-like heads. These are petal-less, instead having ten sepals curving around the top. The actual petals are insignificant and hidden within the flowerhead. Often forms pleasing patches among limestone pavements.
Similar species: None.

▶ MARSH MARIGOLD
Caltha palustris
Family Ranunculaceae

Flowering period: March to August.
Distribution: Widespread everywhere, but less common in arable areas.

Adds a splash of colour to wet meadows, marshes, streams, ditches, riverbanks, flushes and ponds. This creeping perennial is a plant that goes by many names, including May blobs and king cups. Growing to 45cm, the much branching, hairless stems carry large, kidney-shaped leaves that are shiny dark green and toothed, sometimes with a pale mottling. Leaves are mostly at the base of the plant, originating from a fleshy root system.
   Flowers, 10–50mm, have five golden yellow sepals and no petals. These grow on wide branching heads in loose groups at upper end of stems. Flowers are stalked and have fifty to a hundred stamens and one stigma per ovary. This plant used to be hung over farm doorways to ward off witchcraft and as a protection against lightning strikes.
Similar species: None.

▶ LESSER SPEARWORT
Ranunculus flammula
Family Ranunculaceae

Flowering period: June to October.
Distribution: Very abundant throughout the NYM and Dales areas, less common in the lowlands separating these two upland districts. Does not like acid water.

A component of marshes, shallow moving water, ponds and ditches, this native perennial grows to 70cm, is hairless and creeping with narrow, oval or lanceolate leaves. The latter are 10–50mm long, either scarcely toothed or not at all, arranged spirally up the often reddish, slightly branching stem. The leaf base can be rounded, tapered or heart-shaped. Root leaves are stalked, stem leaves not. Stipules are absent.
   Flowers, 8–25mm, are hermaphrodite and grow either solitary or few in number on a branched head at the tip of the stem. Blooms are buttercup-like with five bright glossy yellow petals that are oval to almost circular. There are five equal yellowy-green sepals, numerous stamens and one stigma per ovary.
Similar species: None.

▶ CREEPING BUTTERCUP
Ranunculus repens
Family Ranunculaceae

Flowering period: May to September.
Distribution: Common and widespread throughout.

Found in damp pastures, verges, gardens, alongside reservoirs, indeed anywhere that is grassy. It is a slightly hairy perennial growing from

TOP LEFT: MARSH MARIGOLD. TOP RIGHT: GLOBEFLOWER. MIDDLE: CREEPING BUTTERCUP. BELOW: LESSER SPEARWORT.

rooting runners (hence the name) and reaches between 10–60cm tall. The leaves have three bluntly-toothed lobes giving them an overall somewhat triangular shape in outline. The terminal lobe is stalked, and the leaves as the plant matures typically have white marks on them.

This is the plant that turns 'improved' grasslands into a 'sea' of golden yellow in summer. Flowers can be up to 25mm diameter and occur singly on a grooved stalk. They have five bright yellow petals surrounded by erect sepals that are not bent downwards. The Latin name ranunculus means 'little frog'. All parts of this plant are toxic.
Similar species: BULBOUS BUTTERCUP (*R. bulbosus*) is shorter (up to 30cm) with furrowed stems and similar root leaves with the stalked end lobe. Stem leaves are more deeply divided than *R. repens*. Distinguished from other buttercups by its bulbous tubers and sepals that are turned down. Flowers May to June but prefers drier grassy habitats.

MEADOW BUTTERCUP (*R. acris*) is a tall (up to 100cm) hairy perennial having distinguishing two to seven lobed root leaves that are somewhat rounder in outline than either of the previous two species. Upper leaves are narrow-lobed, the stems having projecting hairs while those on the leaves are flattened. There are no stipules. The hermaphrodite flowers, growing numerous in a branching head from the upper stem, have unfurrowed stalks. Flowers have five rounded petals (6–12mm), erect sepals and golden yellow nectaries. The plant shares similar habitats with R. repens flowering from April to October.

▶ GOLDILOCKS BUTTERCUP
Ranunculus auricomus
Family Ranunculaceae

Flowering period: April to May.
Distribution: Not nearly so abundant as the other buttercups.

This short, scarcely hairy native perennial is an indicator of old established woodland and prefers shady glades and hedgerows, and sometimes (but rarely) old hay meadows. It is distinguished by often having deformed petals, ones of differing sizes, or missing altogether, making the plant appear 'untidy'. The lowermost leaves are divided into three broad lobes that are partially cut along their margins. The stem leaves are narrow,

untoothed and arranged in whorls of four to six. The flowers (15–25mm diameter) are few in number with purple-tinged sepals and petals zero to five in number.
Similar species: MEADOW BUTTERCUP (*R. bulbosus*) see creeping buttercup.

▶ LESSER CELANDINE
Ranunculus ficaria
Family Ranunculaceae

Flowering period: March to May.
Distribution: Very common throughout. This plant seems to succeed virtually anywhere except, that is, the high moorland.

This plant is one of the first indicators that spring has arrived. Found in open woodland, waysides and verges, often forming golden yellow carpets. A hairless perennial growing to 25cm, with stems that angle upwards and bear dark green, almost fleshy, leaves (10–40mm long). These are spirally arranged from the base or up the stem on long stalks and can be heart-shaped, rounded or blunt with shallowly-toothed edge and notched base. Stipules are absent.

The flowers are hermaphrodite and 20–30mm diameter and carried singly on long stalks. There are no bracts. They have eight to twelve narrow, pointed and narrowly oval, shiny yellow petals, three oval sepals and many stamens and stigmas. The petals sometimes turn white with age. This is one of the flowers celebrated in verse by William Wordsworth.
Similar species: The very rare WINTER ACONITE (*Eranthis hyemalis*) is also a spring plant, but possibly a garden escape. It is a low, hairless perennial with solitary flowers that have six oval, golden yellow sepals and a ring of bracts forming a collar immediately beneath the flower. Known from only one or two places in the Dales and slightly more numerous in the NYM and on the magnesian limestones. Flowers January to March.

▶ YELLOW CORYDALIS
Corydalis lutea
Family Berberidaceae

Flowering period: May to November.
Distribution: An introduction that is uncommon but increasing its range on walls near habitation in limestone districts.

TOP: LESSER CELANDINE. BELOW LEFT: GOLDILOCKS BUTTERCUP. RIGHT: YELLOW CORYDALIS.

Also referred to as yellow fumitory, this short (up to 30cm) perennial is a floppy, hairless plant that often tolerates shade. It has leafy, sometimes reddish, stems with pinnately divided feathery leaves. The latter occur as two pairs together with an end leaflet, each leaflet being three-lobed resembling an acorn in shape. Stalks bear up to ten trumpet-shaped bright yellow flowers (12–18mm long) in dense spikes on upper stems. They are two-lipped flowers with a short spur.
Similar species: None.

▌ ROSEROOT
Sedum rosea
Family Crassulaceae

Flowering period: May to June.
Distribution: This stonecrop relation is an arctic/alpine mountain plant known only in the Dales, where it is restricted to crevices and ledges high on the Three Peaks of Craven and some scars in upper Wharfedale.

It is a short (up to 40cm) hairless perennial with glaucous fleshy leaves that are pointed oval and greyish-green in appearance, sometimes tinged red or purple. These grow spirally up the stem, and sometimes grow so densely that the stem is hidden. The leaves are usually toothed towards the end of the lobe, though some may be vaguely so.

Also known as midsummer-men because girls in the past used them to determine whether their loved ones were true. Often patch-forming, the brush-like yellow flowers are four-petalled and grow in flat-topped heads with the female and male reproduction organs on separate plants.
Similar species: None.

▌ LADY'S MANTLE
Alchemilla vulgaris agg.
Family Rosaceae

Flowering period: May to September.
Distribution: One of the more common ssp., especially on calcareous soils. Found throughout the Dales and NYM, less frequent on the magnesian limestones, and absent from the high moors and the VoY.

This is a low-medium (up to 60cm) perennial of grassland and road verges. It has palmately lobed leaves that are slightly dished so that they often hold water after rainfall. Leaves are serrated and not divided to the base. Both stems and the underside of the leaves are densely hairy, the remainder of the plant hairless. Flowers are 3–5mm, growing in loose clusters and noticeable on account of the yellow anthers.
Similar species: Many. This is a very variable and difficult group of plants to differentiate, where accurate separation is only possible by closely studying leaf shapes and size, together with the degree of hairiness. Some ssp. are very rare.

▌ AGRIMONY
Agrimonia eupatoria
Family Rosaceae

Flowering period: June to August.
Distribution: Found throughout the NYM and on the magnesian limestone belt east of the Dales, but less common here and in the Wolds and east coast. Also recorded from the SFNR in South Yorkshire.

This common component of grassy banks, woodland margins and roadsides is a relative of the rose, and not figworts like the mullein of which it resembles a slimmer version. This downy, native perennial has somewhat slender stems growing to heights of 120cm. The short-stalked, pinnate leaves are arranged alternately up the stems, with three to six pairs of toothed leaflets some 15–50mm long. These are grey beneath.

Flowers are hermaphrodite, 5–8mm, and yellow forming a slender spike. Each flower has five oval pointed petals and five pointed sepals equalling them in length. There are up to twenty stamens and one to two stigmas. The plant was once thought to be an effective anti-venom for snakebites.
Similar species: FRAGRANT AGRIMONY (*A. procera*) is very rare and favours acidic soils. It grows in a handful of locations around the NYM, the Washburn Valley and elsewhere in the Dales. It is a larger, sweetly aromatic plant with much larger leaves that are stickily hairy underneath.

▌ TORMENTIL
Potentilla erecta
Family Rosaceae

Flowering period: May to September.
Distribution: Widespread in the NYM and Dales, and recorded also from parts of the Wolds and from Skipwith Common.

TOP: ROSEROOT. BELOW LEFT AND INSET: AGRIMONY. RIGHT: LADY'S MANTLE. BELOW: TORMENTIL.

This native perennial is a common species found in acid grasslands and heaths everywhere, including the high fells, and also on limestone where there is an acid soil or peaty overlay. It is a creeping plant that is downy with slender, branching stems growing to 25cm. Root leaves form a basal rosette, while stem leaves are alternate arranged. These are trefoil and unstalked with three to five leaflets originating from toothed stipules. Each leaflet is 5–20mm long, the lowest leaves long-stalked, upper ones unstalked.

The flowers (7–11mm diameter), are hermaphrodite and grow in loose, branching clusters, resembling tiny buttercups. There are four yellow petals, 3–6mm, slightly notched to give them a heart shape; four spear-shaped sepals obviously separating the petals, are surrounded by a ring of bracts. There are fourteen to twenty stamens and numerous stigmas.
Similar species: TRAILING TORMENTIL
(*P. anglica*) is far less commonplace, growing on light acid soils at lower altitudes. Unlike *P. erecta*, this plant is sometimes found growing in woods. It has larger flowers (14–18mm) that grow solitary with four to five petals. The stems are longer and rooting at leaf axils with some leaves divided into five leaflets. Stem leaves are short-stalked.

▌ SHRUBBY CINQUEFOIL
Potentilla fruticosa
Family Rosaceae

Flowering period: May to July.
Distribution: Very rare. Native only in Teesdale, and anywhere else as an infrequent garden escape.

This downy deciduous shrub favours riverbanks and damp hollows among upland rocks, often forming patches where it grows to heights of 1 metre. It has greyish leaves that are hairy with five, narrow and untoothed leaflets. Yellow flowers (20mm diameter) occur in loose clusters and have five roundish and slightly overlapping un-notched petals and prominent sepals. The plant is dioecious.
Similar species: ALPINE CINQUEFOIL
(*P. crantzii*) is rare, found only in a few places among rocky calcareous grassland and cliffs in the Dales. It has prettier flowers (often orange or brown-spotted) of 10–25mm diameter on a flower stalk arising from the sides of the terminal leaf

rosette. Flowers appear from June to July and have five slightly heart-shaped petals.

SPRING CINQUEFOIL (*P. tabernaemontani*) is less common even than *P. crantzii* with which it shares a similar habitat. Known from just a handful of locations in the Dales and the odd place in West Yorkshire to the east of Leeds. Root leaves have five to seven leaflets of 10–40mm length. Flowers are 10–20mm diameter, appearing April to June.

▌ CREEPING CINQUEFOIL
Potentilla reptans
Family Rosaceae

Flowering period: May to August.
Distribution: Common throughout the lowlands on waste places, verges, bare ground and railway trackbeds on non-acid soils.

This sparsely hairy perennial has trailing stems (slightly reddish) to 1 metre, rooting at leaf nodes. It has palmate leaves having five to seven toothed leaflets. Base leaves are long-stalked. Flowers (16–26mm) are vivid yellow, turning orange toward the centre, growing solitary on long stalks. They have five, heart-shaped petals that are longer than the pointed sepals. There are over twenty stamens with brownish anthers.
Similar species: SULPHUR CINQUEFOIL
(*P. recta*) is a scarce garden escape found in a few dry grassy and waste places in West Yorkshire. This short-medium (to 60cm) hairy plant has somewhat stiffly erect stems carrying leaves with five to seven toothed leaflets, the lowermost ones up to 100mm in length. Stipules are present. The hermaphrodite flowers (20–25mm in diameter) grow in loose clusters and have five barely notched pale yellow petals that are longer than the pointed sepals. Bracts are present. Flowering June to September.

▌ COMMON ROCK-ROSE
Helianthemum nummularium
Family Rosaceae

Flowering period: May to September.
Distribution: Widely found on short limestone grassland.

This pretty flower is a native perennial forming a prostrate undershrub growing to 25cm. Leaves, 5–20mm, grow in opposite pairs on stems and are lanceolate with rounded tip and tapering towards

TOP: COMMON ROCK-ROSE. BELOW LEFT: SHRUBBY CINQUEFOIL. RIGHT: CREEPING CINQUEFOIL.

the base. Stems are scarcely hairy but leaves whitish downy on underside. The stipules are narrow and spear-shaped.

Flowers, 15–25mm, are a golden yellow (rarely white or orange) with five more or less roundish petals, 6–12mm, that overlap and grow one to twelve in number on one-sided spike-like head at tip of stem. There are five narrow sepals and spear-shaped bracts. There is one stigma and many stamens.

Similar species: HOARY ROCK-ROSE (*H.canum*) is a much smaller plant and not very common but can be found in upper Teesdale. It has narrower leaves that are downy and grey above, and smaller (10–15mm across) flowers appearing May to June.

SILVERWEED (*Potentilla anserina*) is a creeping perennial favouring the splash zone along roadsides. It grows to 15cm and has pinnately lobed leaves with three to twelve pairs of leaflets plus a terminal leaflet. These are serrated and light-coloured or greyish on the underside, giving rise to the name. The hermaphrodite flowers are 15–20mm diameter, growing solitary on long stalks. There are five bright yellow oval petals (7–10mm) that are twice the length of the sepals. Flowers May to August.

◗ HERB BENNET

Geum urbanum
Family Rosaceae

Flowering period: May to September.
Distribution: A widespread find on damp soils, in woodland fringes, hedgerows and other shady habitats at lower altitudes.

Sometimes referred to as wood avens, this medium height, native downy perennial usually grows to heights of around 60cm with leaf-like stipules up the stem. The basal leaves are pinnate with three broad-tipped toothed leaflets. The yellow flowers (8–15mm diameter) occur singly or in loose clusters.

Blooms have five oval petals with prominent green, pointed sepals between. The flowerhead is normally quite flat rather than dished or bell-shaped. This species often hybridizes with *G. rivale* to form *G. intermedium*. In the Middle Ages this plant was said to offer protection against evil spirits and witchcraft and became known as the 'blessed plant' for this reason.
Similar species: None.

◗ CROSSWORT

Cruciata laevipes
Family Rubiaceae

Flowering period: April to June.
Distribution: One of the more common members of the bedstraw family, and very abundant throughout. Not found on moorland.

Crosswort is a short native perennial of unimproved grassland and waysides on non-acid soils. Has softly hairy leaves, and stems reaching heights up to 60cm. Individually it is a rather insignificant plant, but it very often forms attractive patches at the base of dry-stone walls. It has elliptical leaves forming whorls of four, like a cross, at intervals up the stem. The honey-scented flowers are minute and easily overlooked. They are pale yellow and form lovely whorls at the base of the leaves.
Similar species: None.

◗ LADY'S BEDSTRAW

Galium verum
Family Rubiaceae

Flowering period: June to September.
Distribution: Common in the NYM, the Dales and on the magnesian limestone corridor and parts of the Wolds.

This delicate plant favours limestone pastures, disused quarries, roadsides and hedgerows. Once used to stuff pillows, hence the name, this native perennial is a low, straggling, practically hairless plant growing to 30cm. The much-branched upright stem carries eight to twelve dark green, linear leaves (6–15mm long) that are untoothed, shiny with margins turned inwards, growing in whorls. Stipules are leaf-like.

Flowers are tiny (2–4mm across) forming a leafy inflorescence and are hermaphrodite and star-shaped with four spreading, bright yellow petals (1–2mm long) joined at the base. There are four stamens and two club-shaped stigmas.
Similar species: None.

◗ MOUNTAIN PANSY

Viola lutea
Family Violaceae

Flowering period: May to August.
Distribution: Fairly common in the Dales on

TOP: MOUNTAIN PANSY. MIDDLE LEFT: LADY'S BEDSTRAW. RIGHT: CROSSWORT. BELOW: HERB BENNET.

upland pastures that are less calcareous, on leached soils or limestone covered with glacial drift.

This mildly calcifuge species is a very attractive native perennial sometimes referred to as the yellow violet. The flower grows solitary on a slender stem of 30cm, from a basal rosette of toothed, spoon-shaped leaves. Can be hairless or hairy with stem leaves that are pinnate lobed on opposite sides of the stem. Stipules are palmate.

The flowers are 15–30mm across with a long spur and petals that are longer than sepals. Petals are normally lemon yellow with darker streaks, but sometimes having upper petals that are blue or purplish.

Similar species: FIELD PANSY (*V. arvensis*) has smaller (10–15mm) cream-coloured (sometimes tinged violet or yellow) flowers, with petals shorter than sepals and leaves that are broad and semi-pinnate. A weed of cultivation, common throughout the NYM and magnesian belt, very rare in the Dales or elsewhere. Flowers April to November.

❱ ROSE OF SHARON
Hypericum calycinum
Family Guttiferae

Flowering period: June to October.
Distribution: Known from West Yorkshire, the NYM and occasionally elsewhere.

This creeping medium (up to 40cm) evergreen undershrub is an occasional garden escape found colonizing waste ground close to habitation. It has opposite pairs of elliptical, dark green leaves and masses of spectacular, exotic-looking yellow flowers. The latter are hermaphrodite and are up to 80mm diameter and have five notched petals and numerous red anthers.

Similar species: None.

❱ TUTSAN
Hypericum androsaemum
Family Guttiferae

Flowering period: June to August.
Distribution: A native shrub scattered throughout the Dales, the magnesian limestones and in the NYM. Sometimes found along bridleways and lanes close to habitation from which it is probably a garden escape.

Also known as sweet amber, this attractive relation of the St John's wort favours woods and hedgerows. It is a hairless perennial growing to 1 metre or so. The often reddish stems are two-winged, woody and branching, with opposite pairs of broad, pointed oval leaves (50–100mm long) that are stalkless and sometimes have reddish veins.

The flowers (12–23mm) resemble a smaller rose of Sharon, and are hermaphrodite with five yellow splayed petals, 6–12mm long, oval and not notched. The heads have a prominent tuft of upright stamens equalling petals in length. There are three stigmas and five sepals, 8–15mm long, that are blunt oval, sometimes reddish. The leaves are aromatic if crushed and the fruit, a red berry, turns glossy black when ripe.

Similar species: STINKING TUTSAN (*H. hircinum*) is a much rarer garden escape introduced from the Mediterranean. Recorded from a few locations in West Yorkshire and the Dales. It has flowers that are larger (30mm) with narrower sepals and stems normally angled bearing narrower leaves.

❱ PERFORATE ST JOHN'S WORT
Hypericum perforatum agg.
Family Guttiferae

Flowering period: July to September.
Distribution: Scattered throughout the Dales, the magnesian limestones and NYM. Also known from the SFNR.

Known as common St John's wort, this native perennial is a plant of hedgebanks, roadsides and unmanaged grassy places. Growing to a height of 50cm the branching stems are upright and woody at the base, and have two raised ribs along their length. Stipules and hairs are absent. Leaves, 10–20mm, are oval or linear with many translucent dots, and paired on the stems.

Hermaphrodite flowers are 17–25mm, and grow numerous in wide branching heads. Flowerheads have five yellow petals, 8–14mm, and are pointed oval with a line of black dots along their margin. Bracts are leaf-like, and the five sepals (also sometimes with black dots), 5–7mm, are spear-shaped. The stamens are numerous and brush-like with three stigmas on long styles.

Similar species: IMPERFORATE ST JOHN'S WORT (*H. maculatum*) is rare in the Dales and scattered in the NYM. It has square stems without

TOP: ROSE OF SHARON. BELOW LEFT: PERFORATE ST JOHN'S WORT. RIGHT: TUTSAN.

wings. The leaves normally have no translucent dots and the petals have black dots over the surface, not the edges. Sepals are blunt, not spear-shaped. Identical flowering period.

SQUARE-STALKED ST JOHN'S WORT (*H. tetrapterum*) is found in damp grassland, beside ponds and rivers. Common to the NYM and Dales, also from SFNR. It has winged stems with semi-clasping leaves that have translucent spots. The 10mm flowers are pale yellow and not black dotted. Identical flowering period.

HAIRY ST JOHN'S WORT (*H. hirsutum*) is a plant of limestone grassland. It differs in being downy. Leaves are elliptical with the usual translucent dots; flowers, 15–20mm across, are pale yellow and sometimes red-veined. The sepals are pointed and edged with black spots. Identical flowering period.

▶ WILD DAFFODIL
Narcissus pseudonarcissus
Family Amaryllidaceae

Flowering period: February to April.
Distribution: Common in NYM where it is known from several valleys, famously including Farndale. Scattered in the Dales and magnesian limestone belt. Unknown elsewhere.

Native perennial still to be found in small quantities in woodlands. It grows to height of up to 50cm with greyish-green grooved leaves all from the base. Flowers are solitary and nodding on hairless, leafless stems. The perianth is formed of six pale yellow outer petals, 35–60mm, with a darker yellow, trumpet-shaped corona as long as petals. Petal lobes are pointed oval and spread apart. Bracts are paper-like and 20–60mm in length. There are six stamens and one style (with swollen tip) within the corona.
Similar species: GARDEN DAFFODIL (*Narcissus agg.*) has several varieties often found planted out in the wild, growing usually near habitation on roadsides, lanes and woodland fringes, but in some cases quite wild locations.

▶ PYRENEAN LILY
Lilium pyrenaicum
Family Liliaceae

Flowering period: June to July.
Distribution: A garden escape that has naturalized in a few scattered localities close to habitation, including Kettlewell and beside Douk Gill in Horton-in-Ribblesdale.

This spectacular perennial bulb grows to heights of 75cm and has leaves that are strap-like, about 8mm wide and up to 450mm long, arranged alternately and spirally up the stem. The beautiful flowers, some 50–60mm in diameter, are yellow with black spots and dashes, the five petals curling back on themselves. There are six stamens with obvious bright orange anthers.
Similar species: MARTAGON LILY (*L. Martagon*) has wider, dark green leaves that are elliptical and arranged in whorls up the stem. Flowers are smaller and mauve or dull pink, dotted and streaked with darker purple. There are some long-established plants in the grasslands at Fountains Abbey. Shares a similar flowering period.

▶ HONEYSUCKLE
Lonicera periclymenum
Family Caprifoliaceae

Flowering period: June to October.
Distribution: Very common.

The sweet-scented honeysuckle is a frequent sight in lowland hedgerows and woods on non-acid substrates. It is a native woody climber growing to 6 metres, which trails over and around other shrubs adding a splash of colour to otherwise drab hedges. The stems may be hairless or downy and twine clockwise, carrying opposing pairs of pointed oval, untoothed leaves (30–70mm long) that are bluish-tinged beneath and may be short-stalked or unstalked.

Flowers, four to thirty in number, form a short-stalked head with bracts shorter than flowers. The hermaphrodite blooms can be yellowish or creamy white, sometimes tinged with purple or red. There are five petals (40–50mm long), the bases of which join to form a trumpet-shaped corolla, with the upper four lobes joined into a broad lip, the lowermost lobe curving backwards. There are five stamens and one stigma with swollen tip.
Similar species: FLY HONEYSUCKLE (*L. xylosteum*) is a planted deciduous shrub that has escaped and become naturalized in a few localities. Not growing quite so high as *L. periclymenum*, it has smaller, yellowish flowers appearing May to June.

TOP AND INSET: WILD DAFFODIL. BELOW LEFT: PYRENEAN LILY. RIGHT: HONEYSUCKLE.

❯ GOOSEBERRY

Ribes uva-crispa
Family Grossulariaceae

Flowering period: March to May.
Distribution: A frequent and widespread native shrub throughout the lowlands, but often reaching an altitude of 300 metres.

This member of the edible currant family can be found growing in woodland, green lanes, older hedgerows and scrub. It forms a straggling bush that can reach heights of 3 metres, though more commonly only half that. It is characterized by spiny stems that bear short-stalked, deeply crenellated palmate leaves, 30–60mm long, with three to five, sharp-toothed lobes.

The bell-shaped flowers appear singly or in drooping clusters of two to sixteen pairs from groups of the leaves. They have five yellowish-green petals edged with red or purple. Fruit are egg-shaped and hairy, green sometimes tinged red and have a tart flavour. The latter are popular in the making of preserves and fruit pies.
Similar species: None.

❯ PINEAPPLE MAYWEED

Chamomilla suaveolens
Family Compositae

Flowering period: May to mid-autumn, though sometimes lasts the whole year.
Distribution: There are few plants so ubiquitous or tenacious. Common throughout the county.

This is an introduced annual originating from Oregon in 1871 which, unusually, seems to thrive on well-trodden ground, disturbed or waste places in the lowlands. Sometimes called simply pineappleweed, this lowly species grows to 20cm, is hairless and pungently aromatic.

The leaves are two to three pinnately lobed and feathery-like, and when crushed they give off a bouquet that some people liken to pineapple. Hmm, well, try it yourself! The rounded, oval or cone-shaped flowerheads have greenish-yellow disc florets only and lacking outer florets common to many species of the daisy family. They grow solitary on long stalks with sepals-like bracts that have pale coloured edges.
Similar species: None.

❯ PELLITORY OF THE WALL

Parietaria judaica
Family Urticaceae

Flowering period: June to October.
Distribution: A very scarce plant for the NYM, Wolds and Dales, scattered on the magnesian belt east of there. Notable colonies exist on cliffs at Fountains Abbey.

This somewhat inconspicuous calcicole plant seems to thrive in impoverished situations, such as church walls, rooting in old mortar. The much-branching, reddish stems are covered in soft hairs. These carry alternatively arranged, pointed and untoothed oval leaves (70mm) with a red central vein. The small (3mm) flowers – male and female on separate plants – are green with yellow stamens. These grow in clusters from the leaf axils and close to stems. The greenish calyx has four teeth.
Similar Species: None.

❯ RED GOOSEFOOT

Chenopodium rubrum
Family Chenopodiaceae

Flowering period: August to October.
Distribution: Not common in the Dales and more widespread in NYM and magnesian limestone belt. Also known from southern Wolds area.

This is an unattractive plant of disturbed ground that is nitrogen-rich, such as manure heaps. Growing to heights of around 60cm, the squarish stems of this native annual are hairless and a touch mealy in appearance, bearing alternate leaves that approximate a diamond in shape with irregular teeth. The many inconspicuous green (sometimes red tinged) flowers are without petals and borne in crowded spikes originating from the upper leaf axils.
Similar Species: SPEAR-LEAVED ORACHE (*Atriplex hastata*) is found along many roadside verges. It has reddening stems with ascending branches. These bear triangular leaves, the basal lobes being at right-angles to the leaf stalk and bracts always toothed. Flowers July to October.

TOP LEFT: GOOSEBERRY. RIGHT: PINEAPPLE MAYWEED. BELOW LEFT: PELLITORY OF THE WALL. RIGHT: RED GOOSEFOOT.

▶ SUN SPURGE

Euphorbia helioscopia
Family Euphorbiaceae

Flowering period: All year.
Distribution: More widespread on the magnesian limestones than either the Dales, NYM or elsewhere. Found on cultivated and waste ground.

This more or less hairless annual is a short (10–50cm) plant forming single upright stems with five upper branches above a leaf cluster. The finely toothed and pointed oval leaves, 15–30mm, are arranged spirally around the stem and are stalkless. Flowers, both male and female on the same plant, are curious in lacking both petals and sepals, the yellowish-green, leaf-like bracts (1–2mm) instead forming a broad umbel.
Similar Species: PETTY SPURGE (*E. peplus*) shares a similar habitat and grows to 30cm. Commonly found among waste places, wall footings, farms and in gardens. The usually unbranched (but not always) hairless stem has oval, untoothed pointed leaves (0.5–3mm) arranged alternately up the stem. The tiny flowers are grouped in threes to form the flowerhead, lack petals but are surrounded by green-coloured bracts. Flowers April to November.

▶ PORTLAND SPURGE

Euphorbia portlandica
Family Euphorbiaceae

Flowering period: April to September.
Distribution: Rare. Normally a plant of clifftops and sand dunes but, curiously, a plant was found in Wharfedale, West Yorkshire. It may still be there.

Like all members of the Euphorbiaceae family this plant is toxic. It is a short (up to 35cm) perennial. The stems are greyish-green, often reddening, and are hairless and branching from the base. The leaves are slenderly oval, up to 34mm in length, and have a prominent mid-rib. They are arranged in opposite rows giving a curious spiral ladder-like appearance. The flowers are not the most prominent feature of this plant, being yellowy-green and very similar to some other spurges in having horned glands, in this case long-horned.
Similar species: This plant is similar to many other spurges, but the leaves of portlandica set it apart from any others in this group.

▶ DOG'S MERCURY

Mercurialis perennis
Family Euphorbiaceae

Flowering period: February to May.
Distribution: Very common plant throughout on calcareous soils, less so on acidic substrates.

A native poisonous perennial traditionally believed to impart an unwelcome blue tint to milk if allowed to grow in pasture or winter feed meadows. This ubiquitous species forms extensive ground-covering in woods, especially beech and ash, and shady roadsides. Growing to 40cm, the downy, unbranched stems have broadly lanceolate, slightly toothed leaves, 30–80mm, in opposite pairs.

Male and female flowers, 4–5mm, are green coloured and grow on separate plants, in stalked tassels from leaf base. Reproduction of the plant is effected more by vegetative means via underground stems, than by seed. There are three sepals with eight to fifteen stamens in male flowers and two stigmas in the female. The latter forms globular seed capsules, 6–8mm, which are broad and hairy.
Similar species: None.

▶ MOSCHATEL

Adoxa moschatellina
Family Adoxaceae

Flowering period: April to May.
Distribution: Common on base-rich soils throughout the Dales and NYM, but scarce elsewhere. Recorded from Middleton Woods, West Yorkshire.

Also known as town hall clock because of the way the inflorescence consists of tiny, radially arrayed flowerheads resembling a clock tower. This native perennial is successfully spread by rhizome. It is a low creeping plant, often overlooked, and found in woods, along hedges and roadsides, and on rocks in semi-shade.

The upright, unbranched stems up to 10cm tall bear pale green, trefoil leaves of 6–25mm. These grow out from the base or two to three together on stems. Hermaphrodite flowers, 6–8mm diameter are greenish and appear in tight heads of five – four facing radially outwards at right-angles to each other with the fifth one pointing upwards. Each flower has two to three

TOP: MOSCHATEL. MIDDLE LEFT: DOG'S MERCURY (MALE FLOWER). RIGHT: PORTLAND SPURGE. BELOW: SUN SPURGE.

oblong sepals, four to five petals joined at base to form a corolla. There are five divided stamens and a similar number of stigmas.
Similar Species: None.

STINKING HELLEBORE
Helleborus foetidus
Family Ranunculaceae

Flowering period: January to May.
Distribution: Rare. Known from a few sites in the Dales (Grass Wood) and Howardian Hills. A garden escape anywhere else.

A perennial of rocky scrubland and dry woods in limestone terrain. It grows to 60cm and has robust, over-wintering stems carrying deeply divided palmate leaves, the lobes being narrow, pointed and finely toothed. The uppermost stem leaves are usually undivided. Flowers, 12–15mm, are petal-less and resemble a lamp shade, with green sepals fringed purply-red. Flowers occur in loose, drooping clusters. The plant is poisonous and has a foetid smell.
Similar Species: GREEN HELLEBORE (*H. viridis*) is very rare for the Dales and scattered in NYM. Has similar palmate leaves but with leaflets either deeply toothed or divided into two to four lobes. The plant grows to half the height of *H. foetidus* and has larger flowers lacking petals, instead having five spreading, dull green sepals. Favoured habitat is accumulated leaf mould in damp woodlands from February to April. The only known specimens are likely to be garden escapes.

TRAVELLER'S JOY
Clematis vitalba
Family Ranunculaceae

Flowering period: July to September.
Distribution: Rare. Known from a few locations in NYM and on the magnesian limestone, probably a garden escape anywhere else. Recorded from SFNR and PCNR, in South Yorkshire and Hull.

This essentially southern species is a tenacious perennial climber, woody and vine-like, growing to as much as 30 metres with pinnate leaves aided by hairless twining stalks. Leaflets, 30–100mm long, form two opposite pairs with one terminal leaflet, all oval or heart-shaped and toothed. Stipules are absent.

Flowers, 20mm, are hermaphrodite and fragrant, and appear numerous in broad branching heads from leaf base or tip of stem. Each has four greenish-white, backwards curving petals with numerous prominent stamens and one stigma. Between September and October the ripe fruits are covered in long grey or whitish hairy plumes, a feature giving rise to the plant's alternative name, old man's beard.
Similar species: None.

BROAD-LEAVED PONDWEED
Potamogeton natans
Family Potamogetonacea

Flowering period: Spring to early autumn.
Distribution: Common plant in Dales, NYM, the Wolds, parts of the VoY and east coast.

An aquatic perennial of slow-moving stretches of water, ponds and ditches. It has submerged, rarely branching stems to 100cm or more in length, bearing 25–125mm floating leaves alternately arranged. These are broad and oval with prominent veins and conspicuous stipules. Plant also has submerged leaves that are ribbon-like in appearance and grooved.

The flowers are small, green, and form a busy spike growing either from leaf axil or stem tip held above the water surface. The flowers are hermaphrodite, bractless and 3–4mm in length. The perianth has four lobes of 1–2mm with four stamens and one stigma.
Similar species: With an identical flowering period, BOG PONDWEED (*P. polygonifolius*) is even more common in similar habitats with smaller, floating leaves often red-tinged, and submerged spear-shaped leaves.

VARIOUS-LEAVED PONDWEED (*P. gramineus*) is very rare and only found in one location in the Dales and NYM. Has oval floating leaves up to 70mm long and submerged leaves with wavy margins. Flowers June to August.

BLACK BRYONY
Tamus communis
Family Dioscoreaceae

Flowering period: May to August.
Distribution: Near its northern limit in Yorkshire. Scattered in Dales but more common in NYM and on magnesian limestone belt. Known from the Wolds and east coast.

This unusual hairless perennial is a relative of the tropical yam, and is fairly commonplace along roadsides where it festoons lowland hedges and woodland margins. Growing to 3 metres this tenacious climber has no tendrils but twines the main stems clockwise. Leaves are long stalked, dark glossy green and heart or arrow-shaped alternately arranged. Flowers are tiny, 3–4mm, pale greeny-yellow with six petals and grow in loose, often branching spikes. This plant is poisonous and bears yellow berries turning red. *Similar species:* None.

▶ STINGING NETTLE
Urtica dioica
Family Urticaceae

Flowering period: June to September.
Distribution: Ubiquitous and common.

This native perennial, known for its armoury of stinging hairs that cover leaves and stems alike, grows to heights of up to 1.5 metres. Seen everywhere on disturbed ground: roadsides, hedgerows, riverbanks, damp woods, ditches, ruined buildings and walls and waste places.

Stems may be creeping or, more normally, upright. These carry opposite pairs of leaves, 40–80mm, that are oval or heart-shaped, sharply toothed with a pointed tip. Stipules are present, but bracts absent. Male and female flowers, 1.5–2mm, are on separate plants; greenish-yellow in whorls of drooping catkins, the male flower with equal perianth lobes, the female unequal. There are four stamens and one feathery stigma. *Similar species:* SMALL NETTLE (*U. urens*) is quite scarce and is a more diminutive plant with a less potent sting. Lower leaves are shorter than stalks. Both male and female flowers are on the same plant.

▶ HERB PARIS
Paris quadrifolia
Family Liliaceae

Flowering period: May to June.
Distribution: Scarce. Known from a few sites in the Dales and NYM and at Bramham Park near Tadcaster.

This handsome but unusual plant is a poisonous native perennial rhizome. Its favourite habitat is damp ground in old and well-established broadleaf woodlands on limestone substrate. The hairless stems bear three to eight (more usually four) prominently veined, untoothed, pointed oval leaves, 60–120mm long, in a whorl on an otherwise leafless stem 15–60cm in length. There are no stipules.

The hermaphrodite flower, 40–60mm across, is solitary and lacking bracts. It is situated at the tip of a stem that is normally longer than the flower. Four (sometimes up to six) green lanceolate spreading sepals form an obvious cross, separating the four (rarely six) insignificant petals. Prominent upright yellow stamens surround a red or reddish-brown ovary that later develops into a black fleshy fruit. The flower gives off a foetid smell that attracts pollinating carrion insects. *Similar Species:* None.

▶ WOOD SAGE
Teucrium scorodonia
Family Labiatae

Flowering period: July to September.
Distribution: Commonplace throughout on dry acid soils.

A plant of rocky scrub, limestone pavements, disused quarries, hedgerows, ledges on cliffs and woodland fringes. The crinkly, vaguely sage-like leaves, 30–70mm, are heart-shaped at the base, blunt toothed and grow in opposite pairs on unbranched, hairy stems reaching heights up to 50cm. Stipules are absent and the leaf stalk is shorter than the leaf blade. Bracts are oval and somewhat shorter than flowers.

The hermaphrodite flowers are greenish-yellow, 9–12mm, growing in leafless, branched spikes from tip of stem. There are five petals, 9–12mm, joined into a corolla with the lowermost lobe the longest and two upper ones noticeably shorter with four protruding dark red or maroon stamens. The forked style carries two stigmas. The five sepals, 4–6mm, are joined into a calyx with pointed oval teeth, the upper ones usually longer. *Similar species:* None.

TOP: HERB PARIS. BELOW LEFT: STINGING NETTLE. RIGHT: WOOD SAGE.

▶ DWARF MALLOW
Malva neglecta
Family Malvaceae

Flowering period: June to September.
Distribution: A very rare plant indeed, known from only one location in NYM and from a handful of sites on the magnesian limestone belt east of the Dales.

This sometimes erect, but usually prostrate, downy annual is a colonizer of waste places and waysides. The stems grow to 70cm and bear scarcely lobed palmate leaves with serrated margins that are smaller than either *M. Moschata* or *M. sylvestris*. These are long-stalked, downy, dark green and deeply veined.

The pretty hermaphrodite flowers (20–32mm diameter) are white or pale pink in colour with lilac veins and have five slightly notched petals. They grow from the leaf axils (one to six in number) on stalks shorter than the leaf stalks. The latter are twice the length of the sepals.
Similar species: None.

▶ WHITE STONECROP
Sedum album
Family Crassulaceae

Flowering period: June to August.
Distribution: Scattered in the Dales, NYM and on magnesian limestone belt, but nowhere that common. Known from Skipwith Common.

A possible introduction to Britain, this mat-forming perennial of walls and rocky places usually grows close to habitation. It bears creeping stems to 15cm with alternate bright green (later turning reddish) cylindrical or oblong, succulent-like leaves. These are 6–13mm (on rare occasions 25mm) long, and flattened on the upper surface. Flowers are star-like 6–9mm across, and form a dense, branching flattened head. Each flower has five pointed white petals and prominent red anthers.
Similar species: HAIRY STONECROP (*S. villosum*) is a downy biennial with 6–12mm alternately arranged leaves that are flattened on the upper surface. Flowers (6mm) are pink and long-stalked. Only in Dales. Similar flowering time.

▶ SPINDLE
Euonymus europaeus
Family Celastraceae

Flowering period: May into June.
Distribution: Scattered in NYM, Dales and on the magnesian limestone belt. A native deciduous shrub/tree found in hedges and woods on calcareous soils. It is the only northern European tree containing a rubber-like substance (gutta percha) in its bark.

Along with three or four other scrubland plants it is often referred to as dogwood. It can grow into a small tree of 6 metres height and has grey and green bark. The four-sided hairless twigs have spear-shaped, slightly toothed bright green leaves (3–10cm long) in opposite pairs. These have serrated margins and turn red in autumn.

The short-stalked flowers are small (1cm diameter) with four oval pointed, greenish-white petals and four joined sepals that are shorter than the petals. The flowers grow in small clusters of three to ten in number. The wood was traditionally used in making spindles, skewers and knitting needles.
Similar species: None.

▶ LILY OF THE VALLEY
Convallaria majalis
Family Liliaceae

Flowering period: May to June.
Distribution: Rare. Locally common in the Dales, less so further east and in the NYM and Wolds. This attractive patch-forming, hairless native rhizome is a species found in ash woodland, scrubby limestone pavement, thickets and hedgerows often in deep shade.

Growing to heights up to 30cm, this perennial has dark green, glossy and broadly elliptical leaves (10–15mm), growing two to a single stem from the base, each with sheathed stalks and obvious longitudinal veins. The hermaphrodite flowers are delicate and sweet scented. These are bell-shaped and nodding, like tiny white lamp shades, growing in one-sided racemes. The flower stems are leafless. Also goes by the names May bells and ladder-to-heaven. The pale orange to red fruits are very poisonous.
Similar species: See COMMON SOLOMON'S SEAL (*Polygonatum multiflorum*).

TOP: DWARF MALLOW. MIDDLE LEFT: WHITE STONECROP. RIGHT: LILY OF THE VALLEY. BELOW: SPINDLE.

❱ COMMON SOLOMON'S SEAL
Polygonatum multiflorum
Family Liliaceae

Flowering period: May to June.
Distribution: Uncommon. Scattered in woods in the Dales, on the magnesian limestone and one or two locations in West Yorkshire.

Native perennial growing to 80cm. The arching stems are smooth and rounded in section and hairless. Leaves are alternate and 50–150mm long, being broadly oval with a pointed tip and untoothed margins. Leaf stalk and stipules are absent. Flowers are two to five in number in branched clusters from the leaf axil. Blooms are hermaphrodite, 9–15mm long, and a greenish white forming a tube that is narrowest in the middle. There are six stamens and a three-lobed stigma.
Similar species: ANGULAR SOLOMON'S SEAL (*P. odoratum*) is nationally rare. Grows in limestone woods and pavement grikes in the Dales. Distinguished by greenish-white bell-shaped flowers that grow solitary or in pairs, and are not waisted.

❱ RAMSONS
Allium ursinum
Family Liliaceae

Flowering period: April to June.
Distribution: Very commonplace throughout.

This is the wild garlic of damp woods, riversides and hedgerows on alkaline substrates where it often completely carpets the ground. It is a hairless native perennial growing 10–45cm tall with broad elliptical leaves from the roots. The flowering stem is triangular in section and leafless. The garlic content of the leaves is said to be good for lowering blood pressure and increasing blood flow.

The hermaphrodite white flowers, 16–20mm diameter, are star-like having six pointed and spear-shaped petals, 8–10mm long. They form an umbel of six to twenty blooms at the tip of the stem. The flower stem is longer than the flower and the bracts are broad and papery. There are six stamens and one stigma with a long style.
Similar species: FEW FLOWERED LEEK (*A. paradoxum*) is much rarer and found in woodland beside rivers. It differs in having a single, narrow leaf and smaller flowers.

❱ WOODRUFF
Galium odoratum
Family Rubiaceae

Flowering period: April and June.
Distribution: Fairly common in the NYM, the Wolds and Dales

This short, at times patch-forming, perennial is almost hairless with unbranching square stems that are upright and grow to 50cm bearing whorls of glossy clasping leaves (2–5cm long) with six to nine pointed lanceolate leaflets. The latter have forward-pointing prickles along their margins. The sweetly-scented, hermaphrodite flowers (4–8mm diameter) grow in a long-stalked lax inflorescence and have four snowy white petals, joined at the base into a corolla.
Similar species: COMMON CLEAVERS (*G. aparine*) frequents shady places: hedgerows, waste ground and woodland fringes. It grows taller than *G. odoratum* and has stickily hairy stems with lanceolate leaves in whorls of six to eight at intervals. Flowers are tiny with four dull white petals, occurring in stalked clusters from leaf axils. Flowers May to September.

❱ HEATH BEDSTRAW
Galium saxatile
Family Rubiaceae

Flowering period: June to August.
Distribution: Very widespread on acid moors and leached calcareous soils and those covered with glacial drift.

This low-short (up to 20cm) hairless perennial is loosely tufted and mat-forming, with narrow spear-shaped leaves arranged in whorls of six to eight at intervals up the stem. Leaf margins are edged with forward-pointing prickles. The white flowers are small, 2–4.5mm, four-petalled and longer than the tube, growing in compact stalked clusters. When young the anthers are yellow.
Similar species: LIMESTONE BEDSTRAW (*G. sterneri*) has backward-pointing prickles on its leaves. Widespread in the Three Peaks area on calcareous soils. Similar flowering time.

FEN BEDSTRAW (*G. uliginosum*) has a scattered distribution in Dales, the NYM and VoY, favouring calcareous wet grasslands and marshes. It has narrow leaves, six to eight in a whorl, with down-turned prickles on angles and ending in a

TOP LEFT: RANSOMS. RIGHT: WOODRUFF. BELOW LEFT: COMMON SOLOMON'S SEAL. RIGHT: HEATH BEDSTRAW.

terminal point. Flowers have yellow anthers. Similar flowering time.

MARSH BEDSTRAW (*G. palustre agg.*) is very common in damp grassland everywhere. Has blunt leaves in whorls of four to five. The hairless stems are rough on the angles, and flowers white with red anthers grow in loose, stalked clusters. Similar flowering time.

NORTHERN BEDSTRAW (*G. boreale*) is rare. Found on higher ground on limestone scars and rocky terrain in the Three Peaks area, and further east in Wharfedale. It is a short, stiff perennial with smooth stems bearing dark green leaves, rough-edged and three-veined in whorls of four. White flowers appear in clusters. Similar flowering time.

KNOTTED PEARLWORT
Sagina nodosa
Family Hippocastanaceae

Flowering period: July to September.
Distribution: Frequent in the Dales (damp sandy or peaty ground) and NYM (forest rides and moorland road edges), scarce anywhere else.

A native perennial growing to heights of 5–15cm, it is the tallest and most showy of the species. It has clumps of needle-like leaves up the stem that, together with undeveloped shoots, gives the appearance of tiny knots at intervals along the hairless stems. Stems each bear solitary white flowers, 5–12mm across. These have five oval green sepals and five oval un-notched petals that are twice the length of the sepals. There are ten stamens and five stigmas with anthers that are off-white or pale yellow.
Similar species: Can perhaps be mistaken for mossy saxifrage or fairy flax.

MEADOWSWEET
Filipendula ulmaria
Family Rosaceae

Flowering period: June to September.
Distribution: Common throughout the county.

A native perennial of damp grasslands (except higher moors), including ditches, roadsides, marshes. Growing to heights of 1 metre, this upright, scarcely branching plant has hairless leafy stems, but dense grey hairs beneath the leaves. The latter are long-stalked, 300–600mm pinnate

with two to five pairs of oval toothed leaflets. Stipules are absent.

The hermaphrodite flowers, 5–10mm, are numerous in dense, shapeless branching heads and are creamy-white and fragrant. The stalk is shorter than the flower. There are five downy sepals that are triangular-shaped and bent backwards, and five petals of 2–5mm. There is one stigma and 20–40 stamens.
Similar species: None.

DOG ROSE
Rosa canina agg.
Family Rosaceae

Flowering period: June to July.
Distribution: Commonplace in lowlands throughout.

A native shrub of waste ground, scrubland, hedgerows and woodland margins. This variable species, growing up to 3 metres, is one of the more familiar plants of roadsides, having arching stems that bear curved thorns and delicately fragrant flowers. Plant is hairless though leaves may have short hairs beneath. Leaves are alternate in two to three pairs of elliptical, pointed and sharply toothed leaflets up to 50mm long.

Flowers may be white or pinkish, 15–25mm diameter (occasionally 50mm) in groups of one to four at the stem end. There are five deeply notched petals of 20–25mm with numerous stamens and many stigmas forming a conical head. In autumn a large (10–20mm) roundish hip appears as an oval or egg-shaped fruit. The sepals fall before the fruit turns a scarlet red.
Similar species: BURNET ROSE (*R. pimpinellifolia*) is much less common and does not grow so tall (50cm). It has cream or pink flowers 20–40mm in diameter. Flowers May to July.

CRAB APPLE
Malus sylvestris
Family Rosaceae

Flowering period: May onwards.
Distribution: Scattered throughout at low altitudes as a component of ancient orchards, hedgerows, green lanes, and woods.

This small (rarely above 8 metres) deciduous native tree is frequently gnarled and bent, with twigs that are often spiny but sometimes not. The

TOP: CRAB APPLE. MIDDLE LEFT: KNOTTED PEARLWORT. RIGHT: MEADOWSWEET. BELOW: DOG ROSE.

leaves (3–4cm long) are short-stalked (10–20mm) rolled, not folded when in the bud, pointed and oval with toothed margins. They are hairless when mature and hairy beneath.

The flowers (30–40mm diameter) occur on short spurs in loose clusters. These are white (sometimes pink) with delicate pink veins and obvious yellow anthers. The small (2.5cm) green (occasionally turning red) fruit are hard and bitter, but they are an important ingredient in hedgerow jelly.
Similar species: The CULTIVATED APPLE (*M. domestica*) enjoys a similar frequency and distribution, usually on the site of old orchards. The twigs are not spiny, the leaves and flowers hairy and the fruit larger (over 3cm diameter).

WILD STRAWBERRY

Fragaria vesca
Family Rosaceae

Flowering period: March to August.
Distribution: Common throughout on calcareous soils. Less likely on moors and virtually absent from arable areas and urban areas.

A low-short (to 30cm) creeping perennial often overlooked among other herbs. Plant propagates through frequently rooting runners. The leaves are bright green and trefoil with pointed teeth, and leaflets paler green with flattened, silky-like hairs. The terminal leaflet is vee-shaped and side leaflets unstalked. The white flowers are 12–18mm across, short-stalked and have five petals separated by obvious, pointed sepals. The fruits are completely covered in seeds and are a miniature version of the cultivated fruit.
Similar species: BARREN STRAWBERRY (*Potentilla sterilis*) is a low hairy perennial with leaves smaller than *F. vesca*. Both leaves and stems have spreading hairs, the stems usually with runners. The white flowers are slightly smaller (10–15mm) with barely notched petals and prominent sepals. Leaves are blunt toothed and smaller, with toothed leaflets of 5–25mm. Favours open woodland and dry grassy places. Flowers February to May.

BRAMBLE

Rubus fruticosus agg.
Family Rosaceae

Flowering period: May to November
Distribution: Ubiquitous and widespread throughout.

Bramble is a common feature on waste ground in summer, in autumn bearing the luscious blackberries favoured in preserves and wine. It is an invasive shrub native to hedgerows, scrubland, roadsides and woodland fringes, but not common on limestone. The sprawling stems can reach lengths of 5 metres and as every blackberry picker knows, are armed with viscious, curved thorns.

It is a woody plant, the long biennial stems rooting wherever they make contact with the ground. They bear prickly alternate leaves with three to five oval, toothed leaflets. The flowers hang in loose clusters and may be white or pink and 20–30mm in diameter, with five widely spaced petals. In autumn the fruit start to swell – red, later becoming glossy black when ripe.
Similar species: There are countless subspecies of this plant. Any attempt at differentiating them is beyond the scope of a book such as this.

BLACKTHORN

Prunus spinosa
Family Rosaceae

Flowering period: March to May.
Distribution: Common throughout.

A deciduous component of hedgerows, roadsides and scrubland. Growing to heights of 4 metres, it spreads via suckers and can form quite dense thickets. The twigs are blackish and can be downy early on. They have 20–40mm leaves that are lanceolate or oval and toothed. Flowers appear usually solitary or in clusters of two to ten. They have five white oval petals with dark red or brown anthers. Flowers appear before the leaves in what is sometimes termed a 'blackthorn winter'.

From August onwards the shrub bears small dark blue plum-like fruits, known as sloes, that are rich in vitamin C and protein but extremely bitter to the taste. They are a constituent of sloe gin. A hybrid of blackthorn with the wild plum produced the modern plum trees. The wood itself is very tough and sometimes used in the manufacture of walking sticks.

TOP: BLACKTHORN. BELOW LEFT: WILD STRAWBERRY. RIGHT: BRAMBLE.

Similar species: WILD PLUM (*P. domestica agg.*) is frequently found in hedgerows in the lowlands. It grows to 10 metres with greyish-brown young branches. These have 20–40mm toothed oval leaves and five-petalled white flowers, 15–25mm appearing in small clusters from April to May. The blue-black fruit is 20–75mm and egg-shaped.

◗ HAWTHORN
Crataegus monogyna
Family Rosaceae

Flowering period: May to June.
Distribution: Common throughout.

A native deciduous shrub growing to 8 metres. It is a pioneer plant which, left unchecked, will rapidly colonize and dominate scrubland. It is the most abundant component of hedgerows, also found in open woodlands. Stems are hairless but bearing spines and leaves that are deeply three to five lobed, each of the latter slightly notched. The hawthorn, or May tree, is a plant of magic and myth; hawthorn sprigs once hung over the fireplace to ward off evil.

Flowers (8–15mm), also known as May blossom, are hermaphrodite with five white, rounded petals, one style and many stamens with prominent brown anthers. Flowers occur in crowded flattened umbel-like clusters. The berries (haws) are dark red and can be used as a constituent in hedgerow jelly.
Similar species: MIDLAND HAWTHORN (*C. laevigata*) is less common. A cultivated species found as an escape in a few scattered localities in the east of our area. It is less thorny and more shade-tolerant with flowers that are a deep red.

◗ ROWAN
Sorbus aucuparia
Family Rosaceae

Flowering period: May to June.
Distribution: Common in all upland areas. Also recorded from Skipwith Common.

Known also as mountain ash, this tree can be found in isolation on the moors, as well as in hedgerows and woodland where it grows to heights of up to 15 metres. It bears pinnate leaves with five to seven pairs of lanceolate toothed leaflets that are green on both sides. The flowers, 8–10mm, are white with five oval, un-notched petals growing in an umbel. The rowan was a tree well known to the Celts for its scented blossom, and to birds for its red berries appearing in late summer and early autumn. As a species it had magico-religious connotations, called alternatively witchen or wiggin tree, and in ancient times it was believed that a loop or cross formed from twigs was sufficient to protect livestock from evil.
Similar species: None.

◗ BIRD CHERRY
Prunus padus
Family Rosaceae

Flowering period: May onwards.
Distribution: Fairly common on calcareous soils.

A deciduous shrub/tree of the rose family often seen in woodland, along riverbanks and in hedges in limestone country, where it grows to 15 metres. The alternately arranged leathery leaves are 50–100mm long, pointed oval and slightly toothed and practically hairless. The five-petalled flowers are 15–30mm and crowded in loose, drooping clusters or spikes ten to forty in number. The small black fruit appear from July onwards.
Similar species: CHERRY LAUREL (*P. laurocerasus*) is a tall evergreen shrub with scarcely toothed lanceolate leaves that are somewhat leathery. The somewhat similar flowers occur in upright spikes rather than drooping as in *P. padus*.

◗ HORSE-CHESTNUT
Aesculus hippocastanum
Family Hippocastanaceae

Flowering period: May onwards.
Distribution: Very common throughout.

An amenity tree originally introduced from the Balkans, since escaped and now has become naturalized in woods, hedgerows and scrub, growing to heights of 25 metres. It has palmate or radiating compound leaves with five to seven variably toothed leaflets 4–19cm long. Flowers are white with a yellow or pinkish spot, have five petals and stand in attractive erect stalked spikes. The fruit, known to children as conkers, are brown when ripe, and contained within a fleshy green outer case that is softly spiked.
Similar species: RED HORSE-CHESTNUT (*A. carnea*) is an introduction and much rarer. It

TOP AND INSET: HAWTHORN. BELOW LEFT: BIRD CHERRY. CENTRE: ROWAN. RIGHT: HORSE-CHESTNUT.

grows to similar heights but has dark pink flowers and darker green leaves.

▶ ELDER
Sambucus nigra
Family Caprifoliaceae

Flowering period: May to July.
Distribution: Widespread and common.

A native deciduous shrub and a frequent component of lowland hedgerows, waste ground and in the woodland understorey. Elder in the past has been surrounded with mystique, always regarded as a witch's tree.

Growing to 10 metres the warty and pithy stems bear pinnate leaves with two to four pairs of toothed, pointed oval leaflets, plus a terminal leaflet. Stipules are usually absent but tiny when present. The wood was once used to make toothed gears for mills. The fragrant flowers, 5mm, are white with yellow anthers, and numerous, growing in more or less flat-topped umbel-like clusters. The fruit makes a fine, port-like wine.
Similar species: DWARF ELDER (*S. ebulus*) is a patch-forming perennial growing to 2 metres. Not as common and usually found beside lanes. Leaves are lanceolate, pinnate with two to four sharp-toothed leaflets. The flowers are also white in umbel-like heads, but have violet anthers. Flowers July to August.

▶ GUELDER ROSE
Viburnum opulus
Family Caprifoliaceae

Flowering period: May to July.
Distribution: Fairly common in the lowlands especially on the magnesian limestone belt and hedgerows in the VoY. Also at Askham Bog. Scattered in the Dales.

A woody deciduous shrub, or small tree, so called because the cultivated variety, the snowball tree, originated from Dutch Guelderland. Growing to heights of 5 metres, it can be found in river valleys, woodland fringes and hedgerows. It also grows in limestone pavements in the Three Peaks area, where it is often semi-prostrate. The barely downy plant has furrowed stems bearing maple-like, palmate leaves with three to five lobes, and somewhat resembling those of ivy.

The flowers, 10mm, are creamy-white and vaguely aromatic, growing in flat umbel-like clusters 50–70mm diameter. Individual blooms have four to five petals, varying in shape and size, and joined at the base. The outermost flowers of the cluster open first and are larger than the inner ones, and lack reproductive organs, being for show only, to attract pollinating insects. In autumn the leaves turn crimson and the plant bears bright red berries.
Similar species: None.

▶ RUE-LEAVED SAXIFRAGE
Saxifraga tridactylites
Family Saxifragaceae

Flowering period: April to May.
Distribution: Abundant in the Dales, scattered in the NYM and rare to non-existent anywhere else.

Also known as the three-fingered saxifrage, the flowers of this annual, unlike most others of the species, are insignificant and short lived. It clings to a tenuous life on stone walls, exposed rocks and scar faces. Growing to 12cm this stickily hairy annual generally produces more than one stem rising from a tuft of, often reddish, almost fleshy leaves. These are untoothed, the upper ones spoon-shaped and lowermost having three lobes. The tiny white flowers, 5mm long, have five notched oval petals with red anthers and grow in loose clusters at the stem tips.
Similar species: None.

▶ MOSSY SAXIFRAGE
Saxifraga hypnoides
Family Saxifragaceae

Flowering period: May to July.
Distribution: Known only from the Dales (abundant along the so-called coal road from Garsdale), where it is commonplace.

This is a plant of rocky terrain, woods and stony grassland on limestone. It is a short, hairy plant forming moss-like cushions. The filamentary leaves are linear and narrow, almost moss-like in appearance and normally have three lobes. The attractive white flowers, few (two to four) in number, grow together on a slender stem, and are 10–15mm across with five oval petals, Sepals are narrow and pointed, the tips sometimes red-tinged.
Similar species: Sometimes confused with KNOTTED PEARLWORT (*Sagina nodosa*).

TOP: GUELDER ROSE. BELOW LEFT: ELDER. RIGHT: MOSSY SAXIFRAGE. BELOW: RUE-LEAVED SAXIFRAGE.

▶ PYRENEAN SAXIFRAGE
Saxifraga umbrosa
Family Saxifragaceae

Flowering period: Flowers in June.
Distribution: Extremely rare. Britain's only extant colony grows in just one location in the Three Peaks area of the Dales.

This attractive perennial is patch-forming with a tufted rosette of fleshy, spoon-shaped leaves with rounded teeth and hairy stalks. Flowers are born on a single reddish, slender stem (20–40cm long) in a loose branching spike with anything up to thirty flowers. The latter have five oval petals. These are white with several red spots and a single yellow spot.
Similar species: LONDON PRIDE (*S. x urbium*) is an introduced perennial naturalized in scattered shady localities close to habitation. It grows to 40cm and has rounded leaves with more obvious teeth.

▶ HEDGE BINDWEED
Calystegia sepium
Family Convolvulaceae

Flowering period: April to July.
Distribution: Common to the magnesian limestones, NYM, but more scarce in Dales and elsewhere.

Known also as bellbine, this introduced hermaphrodite perennial is a tenacious creeper. It grows to 3 metres or more typically among hedgerows, roadsides, walls, fences, ruined buildings and waste places, spreading from a creeping underground stem. Leaves are arrow or heart-shaped, 150mm long, untoothed and arranged spirally around the twining stems.
The hairless stems bear a prolific number of short-stalked, trumpet-shaped flowers (30–55mm) that are solitary at leaf base. There are five white petals of 30–50mm joined into a deep corolla with a calyx formed of five narrow sepals, 9–12mm long, enclosed by two sepal-like bracts. There are five stamens and two stigmas.
Similar species: GREAT BINDWEED (*C. silvatica*) is a tenacious climber with larger (60–75mm) flowers than *C. sepium* and these are sometimes pink or pink streaked. The base of the corolla is usually hidden by inflated sepal-like bracts. Similar flowering time.

HAIRY BINDWEED (*C. pulchra*) is much rarer, a naturalized garden escape usually found close to habitation. It can be distinguished from either of the above in being slightly hairy with flowers that are always pink. Similar flowering time.

▶ YARROW
Achillea millefolium
Family Compositae

Flowering period: June to November.
Distribution: Very commonplace component of grasslands.

Sometimes wrongly confused with umbellifers, but rather than belonging to the carrot family it is a relative of the daisy. Also known as milfoil, this plant grows on roadsides, meadows and hedgebanks, except where peaty soil is present. It is a perennial growing up to 60cm in height and has alternate leaves (50–160mm long) that are pinnate and feathery in appearance.
Flowers grow in flat-topped, umbel-like tight-packed heads, comprising small flowerheads, 4–6mm, that have white ray florets, sometimes tinged pink, with yellowish disk florets. Bracts are dark-edged and scale-like between the florets. Flowers have five stamens and one (two-lobed) stigma but no sepals. The plant is traditionally thought to add a bitter taste and odour to the flavour of milk.
Similar species: None.

▶ SNEEZEWORT
Achillea ptarmica
Family Compositae

Flowering period: July to September.
Distribution: Abundant in the Dales and NYM, less so in the Wolds and anywhere else.

Another relative of the daisy, this native perennial of damp grassy places, marshes and ditches is a plant of medium height (up to 60cm). It has angular and upright, hairy stems bearing alternate linear leaves that have fine saw-tooth margins and are clasping the stem. The flowers, 12–18mm diameter, grow in lax groups that are almost umbel-like in fashion, composite with eight white ray florets and many creamy-white disk florets. The ray florets are irregularly toothed.
Similar species: Yarrow is similar but has smaller flowers.

TOP AND INSET: PYRENEAN SAXIFRAGE. MIDDLE LEFT: YARROW. RIGHT: SNEEZEWORT. BELOW: HEDGE BINDWEED.

▶ COMMON DAISY
Bellis perennis
Family Compositae

Flowering period: All year.
Distribution: Widespread throughout.

This low, hairy perennial is efficiently spread by short rhizomes to the point where it almost takes over from the grasslands in which it is growing. It often invades lawns, but the flower requires a bright day before it will open. The leaves are spoon-shaped and slightly toothed forming a basal rosette from which the flowers rise solitary on leafless stems 3–20cm tall.

The flowerheads, 15–25mm, have yellow hermaphrodite disc florets with strap-shaped white petals, sometimes tipped pink or red. Flowers have oblong, sepal-like bracts 4–6mm long, tiny hair-like sepals, five stamens and one stigma.
Similar species: None.

▶ OX-EYE DAISY
Leucanthemum vulgare
Family Compositae

Flowering period: May to September.
Distribution: Commonplace throughout in meadows, on sunny verges and embankments.

Also known as marguerite or dog daisy, this native perennial grows to heights of 100cm, with slightly hairy, little branched stems and 15–120mm leaves that are quite variable and arranged spirally. The lowermost are usually spoon-shaped or rounded and toothed or lobed, those of the upper stem narrower and clasping.

Flowers are from 25–50mm in diameter with white rays and a central yellow disk of minute hermaphrodite florets, enclosed by bracts. The latter are dark, and papery in appearance around the edges. The sepals are scale-like or absent altogether. There are five stamens forming a tube and a two-lobed stigma on a long style.
Similar species: SCENTED MAYWEED (*Chamomilla recutita*) is a less common on disturbed ground. It has bristle-tipped, finely divided leaves and 10–25mm flowers with rays turned down and bracts that are tinged greenish-white. Flowers June to September.

▶ FEVERFEW
Tanacetum parthenium
Family Compositae

Flowering period: June to September.
Distribution: Scattered throughout the NYM, Wolds, the Dales and at SFNR. More widespread on the magnesian limestones.

A daisy-like, short-medium height (up to 50cm) downy and quite aromatic perennial, found growing in waste places, roadsides, and on walls, usually close to habitation. Leaves are pinnately lobed and alternately arranged. Flowers, 10–25mm in diameter, have white rays, occasionally absent, and yellow disk florets growing in flat-topped, umbel-like clusters.

Feverfew was traditionally used in the treatment of ailments such as arthritis and migraines, and now appears to offer hope in combating leukaemia thanks to parthenolide, a substance found in the plant.
Similar species: None.

▶ BLADDER CAMPION
Silene vulgaris
Family Caryophyllaceae

Flowering period: May to September.
Distribution: Rather scarce in the Dales and scattered in the Wolds and NYM, confined mainly to field margins, wasteland and roadside verges. Known from the Hull area.

This perennial component prefers uncultivated grassy places on neutral or alkaline soils, growing to a medium height (to 80cm). The hairless stems are greyish in appearance. All shoots bear flowers and can be woody at the base. Leaves are pointed, lanceolate or oval, and sometimes have wavy margins.

The fragrant flowers of this semi-sprawling plant are either male or female and smaller than either *S. maritima* or *S. alba*, growing in loose clusters. They are white with five deeply divided petals joining and contained within an inflated and greenish calyx that is obviously bladder-like.
Similar species: See SEA CAMPION (*S. maritima*).

TOP AND INSET: OX-EYE DAISY. MIDDLE LEFT: FEVERFEW. RIGHT: BLADDER CAMPION. BELOW: COMMON DAISY.

▶ WHITE CAMPION
Silene alba
Family Caryophyllaceae

Flowering period: May to October.
Distribution: Fairly common on magnesian limestone belt, but less so in Dales, VoY, the NYM and Wolds.

A native perennial growing to 80cm tall and found typically in hedgebanks, roadsides and grassy places. It is a much branching and stickily hairy plant with oval, or spear-shaped untoothed leaves, 30–100mm, arranged in opposite pairs up the stem.

Flowers are 25–30mm across, white with five deeply divided petals growing few in number on branching heads. Male and female flowers are on different plants: male with ten stamens and female having five stigmas. The calyx tube has five narrow sepal teeth of 23–30mm that are lanceolate and blunt. Sometimes forms a pink hybrid with *S. dioica*.
Similar species: A less common white variant of RED CAMPION (*S. dioica*).

▶ SEA CAMPION
Silene maritima
Family Caryophyllaceae

Flowering period: May to September.
Distribution: Rare. Only on a few limestone screes and scars in the Three Peaks area and at SPNNR.

This is a hairless native perennial typically forming cushion-like growths with few flowering stems. The prostrate plant can cover an area from a few centimetres to nearly 1 metre. It has oval, grey-green leaves that are somewhat fleshy. The short-stalked, white flowers are 15–25mm broad, growing in clusters that are few in number. Each are comprised of five overlapping petals (broader than in *S. vulgaris*) contained in an inflated calyx that is veined with pink. The sepal teeth are broad and pointed.
Similar species: See BLADDER CAMPION (*S. vulgaris*).

▶ GREATER STITCHWORT
Stellaria holostea
Family Caryophyllaceae

Flowering period: April to June.
Distribution: Common throughout on all but acidic soils.

A straggly plant known also as adders' meat, this native perennial of woods, field margins, waysides and hedgerows grows to 50cm tall, with square, somewhat brittle stems. These stems have 40–80mm long and grass-like, stalkless lanceolate leaves in opposite pairs, which are somewhat bluish and rough-edged.

The flowers are 20–30mm diameter, long-stalked and white, with five petals each divided to over halfway. There are ten stamens with orange anthers, three stigmas and five short (6–9mm) sepals that are pointed and prominent. The latter are not conspicuously veined as in *S. graminea*.
Similar species: LESSER STITCHWORT (*S. graminea*) with 5–12mm flowers and sepals equalling length of petals. Flowers May until August but prefers ungrazed grassland very rarely on calcareous soils.

WOOD STITCHWORT (*S. nemorum*) is a short perennial with 12–14mm flowers. Flowers have deeply divided petals twice the length of the sepals. Stems are hairy all around with leaves that are shorter and broader than *S. holostea*. Grows in damp woods May to July.

▶ COMMON CHICKWEED
Stellaria media
Family Caryophyllaceae

Flowering period: All year if conditions are favourable.
Distribution: Common everywhere and one of the few species to benefit from agriculture.

A plant of grasslands and waste ground everywhere, including cultivated land. This, often prostrate, native annual grows up to 40cm and is distinguished by two lines of hairs down the slender, much branching stem. The latter bears oval pointed leaves, 3–25mm, that are untoothed and paired, the lowermost long-stalked and the upper ones not at all. Stipules are absent.

The hermaphrodite flowers are small (6–12mm) and insignificant, with five deeply-lobed white petals that are shorter than the sepals, the latter having a ragged, papery edge to them. There are five (rarely eight) stamens and three stigmas. Bracts are present.
Similar species: BOG STITCHWORT (*S. alsine*) has square stems with unstalked leaves. Flowers are smaller, 4–6mm diameter, with very narrow petals shorter than sepals. It is a very frequent

TOP LEFT: WHITE CAMPION. RIGHT: SEA CAMPION. BELOW LEFT: COMMON CHICKWEED. RIGHT: GREATER STITCHWORT.

member of the waterside plant community and in marshes or flushes from May to August.

FIELD MOUSE-EAR
Cerastium arvense
Family Caryophyllaceae

Flowering period: April to August.
Distribution: Scarce and scattered on base soils throughout the Dales (rare), VoY and NYM in hedgebanks and riversides.

This low, slightly-branching perennial (up to 10cm) has vaguely hairy stems carrying narrow, lanceolate leaves arranged in opposite pairs, and that do not taper at the base. Stipules are present. The flowers (12–20mm diameter), growing solitary or two to three in number at stem tips, have five deeply divided white petals twice the length of the sepals, the latter joined at the base. Sepals reddened at the tips.
Similar species: COMMON MOUSE-EAR (*C. fontanum*) is widespread in grasslands everywhere. A short (to 30cm) perennial with non-flowering leafy shoots. Has lanceolate greyish-green leaves are covered in fine hairs. Flowers (5–11mm diameter) have five white, deeply divided petals equalling the length of the sepals, the latter having white margins. Flowers April to November.

SPRING SANDWORT
Minuartia verna
Family Caryophyllaceae

Flowering period: May to September.
Distribution: Rare. Found only in the Dales on lead mine spoil heaps, particularly in upper Wharfedale.

This prostrate and mat-forming perennial is one of the few lead-tolerant species and as such is often known as leadwort. It frequents short grassland, scar ledges, scree and rocks in limestone. The stems are downy and bear three-veined, linear leaves in whorls at intervals on the stem. The flowers, 8–9mm, have five white pointed, oval petals slightly longer than the prominent sepals. The anthers are a delicate pink. The plant is often found in conjunction with another lead-tolerant plant, alpine pennycress.
Similar species: YORKSHIRE SANDWORT (*Arenaria norvegica ssp. anglica*) is alternatively known as Arctic or English sandwort. It is very rare, known only from the upper Ribblesdale area, and one unsubstantiated location in Littondale. It is a tufted perennial with larger (8–12mm across) flowers with yellow anthers instead of pink. Leaves are somewhat fleshy and oval rather than the more linear form of *M. verna*. It flowers from June to August on bare ground – among rocks and tracks, in limestone country, where it will be found in humus filled hollows.

SNOWDROP
Galanthus nivalis
Family Amaryllidaceae

Flowering period: January to March.
Distribution: A garden escape common throughout.

The delicate white flowers are one of the first harbingers of spring. It has become naturalized mostly on roadsides and near habitation, but not always so, as they may also be found in damp woods, meadows, and beside shady streams and riverbanks. It is a low perennial with narrow, keeled greyish leaves. The flowers (20–25mm) grow singly and nodding on leafless stems, and when fully opened have three outer white petals and inner ones that are white tipped with green. The anthers are green.
Similar species: SUMMER SNOWFLAKE (*Leucojum aestivum*), a short, tufted perennial with bright green leaves, is rare, known from a few locations in West Yorkshire. The flowers have white petals (15–20mm) tipped green and occur in nodding clusters of three to six blooms. Usual habitat is damp grassy places from April to May.

WOOD SORREL
Oxalis acetosella
Family Oxalidaceae

Flowering period: April to May.
Distribution: Widespread and prevalent everywhere in ancient or well-established woods.

This prostrate, creeping perennial prefers shady places on bankings and beside streams. Leaves are bright green and shamrock-like, formed from three heart-shaped leaflets that fold in on each other after dusk and during dull or wet weather. The leaves are occasionally used in salads but consumption in excess is toxic.

TOP: SPRING SANDWORT. MIDDLE LEFT: FIELD MOUSE-EAR. RIGHT: WOOD SORREL. BELOW: SNOWDROP.

The hermaphrodite flowers are a delicately purple-veined white, or lilac white and solitary, rising from the base of the plant on leafless upright stems, from 5–20mm tall. Each bloom is 5–30mm across with five blunt sepals and five equal petals carrying ten stamens and half as many stigmas. When not fully open the flowers appear cup-shaped, but fully displayed are similar to wood anemone though not as large.
Similar species: See WOOD ANEMONE (*Anemone nemorosa*).

▶ BOGBEAN
Menyanthes trifoliata
Family Menyanthaceae

Flowering period: April to June.
Distribution: Scarce with special protected status. Scattered in the Dales, on the magnesian limestone belt, the NYM and Wolds. Confined to unpolluted pools, bogs and marshland.

This rhizome, also known as buckbean, is a native aquatic perennial. The plant creeps from a submerged rhizome and may form dense patches on the water surface. The leaves are conspicuously held above water, and are unusual in being divided into three leaflets with the leaf stems sheathing each other. An infusion of the dried leaves was believed to relieve headaches.
    The unusual and pretty blooms rise solitary on a single stem to form a striking spike. Flowers have five petals forming a corolla and are white with pink edges. The lobes are fringed with white hairs to give the flower its unique, furry-looking appearance.
Similar species: None.

▶ EYEBRIGHT
Euphrasia officinalis agg.
Family Scrophulariaceae

Flowering period: June to October.
Distribution: Very abundant in hill country of the NYM and Dales, less so in South Yorkshire and elsewhere.

A beautiful little flower in miniature, best appreciated by getting down on the knees with a magnifier. This short, creeping hairy annual is a semi-parasite found in grassy places and heaths. With a height up to 15cm, this well-branched plant carries leaves that are mostly oval or oblong and deeply toothed, the upper stem leaves either spiralling or in equal pairs.
    Flower are 5–8mm, grow in leafy spikes. These are white streaked and tinged with purple and having a yellow blotch in the throat. There are four sepals, 3–6mm, joined to form a calyx with pointed teeth. Bracts are leaf-like but small. Five petals join at the base to form a corona, with the lobes notched. The three lower petals are longer. There are four stamens and one long-stalked stigma with a bulbous tip.
Similar species: LARGE-FLOWERED EYEBRIGHT (*E. rostkovoana ssp. montana*) is much scarcer and found in a few isolated damp pastures in upper Wharfedale.

▶ WHITE DEAD-NETTLE
Lamium album
Family Labiatae

Flowering period: March to November.
Distribution: Very abundant on the magnesian limestone belt, less common further west and fairly common in the NYM, VoY and the Wolds.

This softly hairy, native perennial is a feature of waysides, road verges and waste ground. It is faintly aromatic with unbranched, angled stems carrying heart-shaped, toothed leaves resembling those of the common stinging nettle. Leaves are 25–120mm growing in pairs, the leaf stalk shorter than the blade.
    Flowers are white and two-lipped, in whorls at the base of the upper leaves. They have five sepals of from 9–12mm length, forming a tube with slender teeth. Five petals, 20–25mm long have bases forming a tube. The upper two lobes are joined and hood-like in appearance. The lowest lobe is large and turned back, the two side lobes toothed. The four stamens are partially hidden beneath the 'hood'. There are two stigmas on a long, forked style.
Similar species: SPOTTED DEAD-NETTLE (*L. maculatum*) is a less widespread garden escape that has colonized waysides and woodland fringes. The leaves are often vaguely spotted and flowers pink or pale purple.

TOP: EYEBRIGHT. BELOW LEFT: BOGBEAN. RIGHT: WHITE DEAD-NETTLE.

▶ BLACK NIGHTSHADE
Solanum nigrum
Family Solanaceae

Flowering period: July to October.
Distribution: Rare for Dales and scarce on magnesian limestones and elsewhere. Absent from NYM.

A low-short (up to 50cm) annual of waste places, hedgerows and the fringes of arable fields. The plant may be either downy or hairless and has pointed oval leaves, toothed or wavy-lobed, on blackish tenacious stems. The flowers are similar to those of the potato and hang in loose drooping clusters. They have five white petals, turned back at the tips, with a prominent column of yellow anthers. The poisonous fruit appear in autumn and are green first, turning glossy black.
Similar species: See BITTERSWEET (*S. dulcamara*).

▶ ENCHANTER'S NIGHTSHADE
Circaea lutetiana
Family Onagraceae

Flowering period: June to September.
Distribution: Abundant throughout NYM, the Dales and on the magnesian limestone belt. Also known from SFNR in South Yorkshire and in the Hull area.

This slender native perennial of shady waysides and damp woods can grow so prolific as to be patch-forming. It is an insignificant looking plant until one examines it closely, to find the tiny two-petalled flower is quite attractive. It is a downy plant with stems growing to heights of 20–60cm. The paired leaves, 40–100mm long, are oval pointed or vaguely heart-shaped, the lowermost short-stalked. The stem has swellings at leaf base.
 The delicate, hermaphrodite flowers are 4–8mm, and numerous in a loose, leafless elongated spike. There are a few bracts at the base of the latter. The twin white or pinkish petals are divided to halfway. Twin sepals are 2–3.5mm long joined at base into short tube. There are two stamens and a two-lobed stigma. This plant is perhaps better known for its burred fruits that cling tenaciously to walking socks.
Similar species: None.

▶ NEW ZEALAND WILLOWHERB
Epilobium brunnescens
Family Onagraceae

Flowering period: July to August.
Distribution: This perennial was introduced into Britain as a rock garden plant in 1908 and is now naturalized and widespread in upland districts (up to over 360 metres) of the Dales and NYM.

It is a prostrate plant finding a niche along stream banks, among mossy stones, in damp hollows, damp walls, wheel ruts and forest rides. The almost hairless plant has creeping stems with paired, almost fleshy, short-stalked leaves that are rounded and scarcely toothed. As the plant matures the foliage often becomes brown, or takes on a bronzy sheen. The tiny (4mm) flowers are held aloft on lengthy stalks typical of willowherbs and appear solitary on slightly drooping stalks. They are white or pale pink, often refusing to open on dull days. The four petals are deeply notched like most other willowherbs.
Similar species: None, though bog rosemary is sometimes mistaken for this plant.

▶ WOOD ANEMONE
Anemone nemorosa
Family Ranunculaceae

Flowering period: March to May.
Distribution: Commonplace on all soils throughout, especially in NYM, the Dales and the east coast and Wolds.

The wood anemone, or windflower, is one of our prettiest springtime flowers, a common sight in shady places. Although really a native woodland plant, it also copes with unimproved grassland where the old tree cover has since been removed, for instance in the grikes of limestone pavement.
 It is a hairless perennial growing up to 30cm tall with three short-stalked stem leaves growing in a whorl beneath the flower. The leaves are 20–40mm long, and deeply divided palmately-lobed, the lowermost being long-stalked. Root leaves appear after the flowers and are similar in appearance.
 The delicate flowers, which may be white, pink or lilac, are hermaphrodite and solitary cup-shaped, 20–40mm across. These have six to twelve hairless sepals and six pointed oval petals with 50–70 stamens and one stigma per ovary.

TOP: WOOD ANEMONE. MIDDLE LEFT: BLACK NIGHTSHADE. RIGHT: ENCHANTER'S NIGHTSHADE. BELOW: NEW ZEALAND WILLOWHERB.

The perianth has five to nine equal segments that are oblong or elliptical.
Similar species: Sometimes confused with WOOD SORREL (*Oxalis acetosella*).

WHITE WATER-LILY
Nymphaea alba
Family Ranunculaceae

Flowering period: July to August.
Distribution: Very scarce. Known from a scattering of sites in West Yorkshire, the NYM and the magnesian limestones. Very rare for the Dales, known from a disused quarry in the Three Peaks.

This aquatic native perennial rhizome is found in the occasional pond. The floating, glossy green leaves, 100–200mm, are almost circular with the base forming a deep cleft with lobes not overlapping. Hairs are absent, stipules present and leaf stalk up to 3 metres long. The leaves form a wonderful backdrop for the blooms of this beautiful plant.

Flowers are few in number, hermaphrodite and cup-shaped, some 50–200mm across, white (sometimes tinged pink or yellow) with 20–25 spirally arranged petals. There are numerous stamens and stigmas forming radiating lines on top of the ovary and four, spear-shaped whitish sepals.
Similar species: None.

POND WATER CROWFOOT
Ranunculus peltatus
Family Ranunculaceae

Flowering period: May to August.
Distribution: Very scarce and rare in the Dales. Known from a few scattered locations in the NYM and elsewhere.

A very variable native annual or perennial and an infrequent component found in shallow ponds and slow-moving water. The hairless stems carry roundish, shallowly-divided somewhat succulent-like floating leaves (20–30mm diameter) and more thread-like, finely divided submerged leaves. The flowers (10–20mm) are white with yellow anthers matching the centre of the five-petalled flower and are carried on a stem that is longer than the leaf stalk.
Similar species: There are several other, mostly rare and difficult to separate species.

BANEBERRY
Actaea spicata
Family Ranunculaceae

Flowering period: May to July.
Distribution: Rare. In Britain this plant has a restricted range, being confined to a narrow east–west corridor at this latitude. Found infrequently in the Dales and NYM, but also scattered in the Wolds. Also recorded from near Tadcaster.

A plant that favours calcareous terrain, baneberry can be found growing on ledges on limestone scars or in the grikes of limestone pavements. It is a medium (to 65cm) height perennial, noticeably foetid, with glabrous upright stems. The latter carry two trifoliate root leaves or two pinnately lobed long-stalked leaves. The leaflets are pointed oval and deeply toothed.

The white hermaphrodite flowers occur in a dense but pretty stalked oblong raceme, sometimes growing axially but more usually terminal. Each individual bloom has four to six white petals and four obvious white stamens. There are three to four (sometimes six) sepals that are whitish and blunt. The fruit is a large glossy black berry which is quite poisonous.
Similar species: None.

GRASS OF PARNASSUS
Parnassia palustris
Family Parnassiaceae

Flowering period: June to September.
Distribution: Fairly common in the Dales, scattered in the NYM and rare anywhere else. Recorded from near Kippax east of Leeds.

Not a grass at all this, but an attractive plant with delicate white flowers. It is a hairless native perennial and a fairly commonplace occurrence in damp grassland and flushes. The plant forms a rosette of heart-shaped leaves with solitary 15–30mm flowerheads appearing on a single stem having one clasping leaf.

The flowers, vaguely smelling of honey, have five white petals delicately streaked with grey, separated by five spear-like sepals. The fringed stamens combine to make this a stunningly beautiful flower. Its name is derived from Mount Parnassos, a Greek mountain that was home to the mythological muses.
Similar species: None.

TOP LEFT: WHITE WATER-LILY. RIGHT: POND-WATER CROWFOOT. BELOW LEFT: BANEBERRY. RIGHT: GRASS OF PARNASSUS.

◗ COMMON SUNDEW
Drosera rotundifolia
Family Droseraceae

Flowering period: June to August.
Distribution: Abundant in NYM and Dales, but scattered in West Yorkshire and scarce anywhere else. Recorded from the VoY and Skipwith Common.

Also known as the round-leaved sundew, this curious insectivorous perennial is one of three species of British sundew. Favoured habitat is the peaty soils on wet heaths, sphagnum bogs and moorland. Growing to 15cm, it forms a rosette of round, reddish spoon-shaped leaves, from the centre of which rises a single stem, up to 25cm tall, carrying the diminutive white blooms.

    The hermaphrodite flowers are most often seen in the bud state, but when fully open are 5mm diameter with five oval petals in a short spiked cluster. There are five-toothed sepals almost as large as the petals, five stamens and three deeply-forked stigmas. The unique feature of this, and other sundews, is the fleshy leaves, which are fringed with fine sticky hairs. These curve inwards to snare small insects, the leaves then secreting a digestive liquid.
Similar species: None.

◗ CUCKOO FLOWER
Cardamine pratensis agg.
Family Cruciferae

Flowering period: April to July.
Distribution: Common to the Dales, VoY, the NYM, West Yorkshire and Skipwith Common.

A very profuse member of the crucifers. Also known by the name of lady's smock, this native perennial thrives in damp grassland, ditches, poorly drained land and beside streams. The hairless stems grow to 15–60cm with root leaves forming a basal rosette. Leaves are narrowly pinnate, the root leaves having three to four pairs of acorn-shaped leaflets, the upper stem leaves bearing narrow, lanceolate leaflets.

    The attractive flowers (12–21mm diameter) are hermaphrodite having four white, mauve or lavender-lilac petals that are roundish and slightly overlapping with yellow anthers. They occur in loose clusters of between seven and twenty blooms. There are four to six stamens and one stigma.

Similar species: WAVY BITTERCRESS (*C. flexuosa*) differs in that the flowers have six stamens instead of four. Wavy stems rising from an open rosette. It has fewer leaves each divided into thirteen to fifteen leaflets. Favours rocks and damp woodlands from April to September.

◗ COMMON SCURVY-GRASS
Cochlearia officinalis
Family Cruciferae

Flowering period: April to August
Distribution: Scattered throughout the Dales and along the east coast.

This 5–50cm high native biennial or perennial can be seen along streams in the Dales, ledges and boulder-clay grasslands on the coast. The hairless stems are low but angled upwards and bear heart-shaped, fleshy leaves. Those growing from the base have long stalks, the uppermost leaves loosely clasping the stem. Stipules are absent.

    The fragrant hermaphrodite flowers (8–10mm) are white (rarely tinged lilac) and grow in lax heads at the stem tips. They have four un-notched and widely-spaced oblong petals, four obvious green sepals, six stamens and one stigma. Flower stalk is 4–7mm in length.
Similar species: DANISH SCURVY-GRASS (*C. danica*) is less common and found along roadsides with smaller white, but more usually lilac or pink, flowers and mostly long-stalked stem leaves. Flowers from January to September.

◗ HOARY WHITLOW-GRASS
Draba incana
Family Cruciferae

Flowering period: June to July.
Distribution: Nationally rare. Found only on screes, scar ledges, cliffs and limestone pavements mainly in the Three Peaks, around Malham, and in Teesdale.

Sometimes also known as twisted whitlow-grass, this native annual or biennial grows to 45cm. The stiff and leafy stems are hairy, almost downy, and rise from a rosette of almost fleshy, oval pointed toothed leaves, the stem leaves alternate and slightly clasping. Flowers, 8–10mm, are white, with four slightly notched petals and yellow anthers. The fruit pods, when ripe, are twisted hence the plant's alternative name.

TOP LEFT: COMMON SUNDEW. RIGHT: CUCKOO FLOWER. MIDDLE: HOARY WHITLOW-GRASS. BELOW: COMMON SCURVY-GRASS.

Similar species: WALL WHITLOW-GRASS
(*D. muralis*) has smaller (2–3mm) white flowers
with un-notched petals and shorter stems with
rounded and toothed leaves clasping the stem.
Shares similar habitat preferences but is far
less common.

▶ WILD RADISH
Raphanus Raphanistrum
Family Cruciferae

Flowering period: May to September.
Distribution: Absent from the Dales, scattered
elsewhere.

This medium (up to 60cm) native annual is found
on arable and waste land, roadsides and verges
with neutral to acid soils. The roughly hairy,
hardly branching stems bear pinnate leaves with
one to five pairs plus a larger terminal leaflet. The
latter have wide-spaced lobes with toothed
margins. The teeth of the upper leaves are blunt,
with stipules absent.

The hermaphrodite flowers (15–22mm
diameter) are more usually white with darker
veins but can be lilac or even yellow, growing on a
10–50mm long stalk. They have four elongated oval
petals (12–20mm) with four 5–10mm long upright,
red-tinged sepals, six (four long, two short) stamens
and one stigma. There are no bracts.
Similar species: See CHARLOCK (*Sinapsis
arvensis*).

▶ GARLIC MUSTARD
Alliaria petiolata
Family Cruciferae

Flowering period: April to August.
Distribution: Abundant on the magnesian
limestones, in the Dales and NYM but no higher
than around 300 metres. Known also from SFNR.

Jack-by-the-hedge to some people, this
undistinguished member of the cabbage family
is a prolific component of roadsides, woodland
margins and waste ground. It is an upright,
aromatic native perennial, or biennial, with
hairless stems growing to heights of 1 metre with
30–120mm leaves. These are heart or triangular-
shaped, sharply toothed, and arranged spirally
around the branching stems. Upper leaves are
long-stalked, the lowermost short-stalked.

The hermaphrodite flowers are white with no

bracts. They form an elongated head containing
up to thirty blooms of 5–10mm. These have four
petals of 4–6mm, brilliant white and rounded with
a stalk-like base. The four sepals, 2.5–3.5mm, are
oval and greeny-white. There are six stamens and
one stigma. The seed pods are long and slender.
Similar species: None.

▶ HAIRY BITTERCRESS
Cardamine hirsuta
Family Cruciferae

Flowering period: February to November.
Distribution: Ubiquitous throughout in dry
situations: disturbed ground, pavements, the base
of walls, waste places and roadsides.

This native annual grows to heights of 20cm with
hairy stems rising from a compact rosette of
pinnately lobed leaves. Each of the latter has three
to seven pairs of oval, pointed leaflets. Stem leaves
are similar, but fewer and smaller. The flowers
are white and less than 5mm across (usually
2–3.5mm), four-petalled with four stamens.
A feature of this plant is that the young erect seed
pods often stand higher than the unopened flowers
and are more obvious than the stamen.
Similar species: WAVY BITTERCRESS
(*C. flexuosa*) grows a little taller (30cm) and is a
biennial. The principal distinguishing feature is the
wavy stems and seed pods do not stand higher
than flowers. It flowers April to September in
damp grassland and stream banks. It is more
common in the western Dales than *C. hirsuta*.

▶ SEA ROCKET
Cakile maritima agg
Family Cruciferae

Flowering period: June to September.
Distribution: Uncommon. A plant of sand and
shingle. Scattered along the east coast driftline.

A low-growing (to 45cm) annual that is distinctive
by its succulent-like leaves. The upright-
branching hairless stems carry fleshy, linear
to pinnately lobed spirally-arranged leaves
(30–60mm long) lacking stipules. The uppermost
leaves have few or no lobes with only the lower
ones possessing a (short) stalk.

The pretty hermaphrodite flowers are white,
sometimes pink, lilac or purple, growing numerous
in a crowded spike at the stem tip. Flowerheads

TOP LEFT: GARLIC MUSTARD. RIGHT: SEA ROCKET. BELOW: WILD RADISH. RIGHT: HAIRY BITTERCRESS.

are up to 12mm diameter with four petals (6–12mm long), four sepals (3–5mm long), six stamens and one stigma. Bracts are absent.
Similar species: None.

▶ SWEET CICELY
Myrrhis odorata
Family Umbelliferae

Flowering period: May to June.
Distribution: Commonplace in rough grasslands and alongside roads everywhere.

An introduction from southern Europe easily distinguished from other members of the carrot family by its distinctive aniseed aroma. This tall (to 1 metre) perennial has upright stems that are grooved and hollow with short hairs. The leaves, growing from the base or alternately up the stem, are 300mm long, divided two to three times, the lobes oblong and toothed. The leaves are quite often randomly flecked, as if having had milk spilled upon them. There are no stipules.

Flowers, 2–5mm, are hermaphrodite in the same inflorescence. The latter contain many heads of 10–50mm across, with individual flowers having five white oval, deeply divided petals (1–3mm), with five minuscule sepals. There are no bracts beneath the inflorescence. Petals are equal in length except on the outer flowers, and there are five stamens and two very slender stigmas.
Similar species: COW PARSLEY (*Anthriscus sylvestris*) is a very common component of grasslands everywhere. It differs in often having purple or purple-blotched stems that are hairless below and downy above. The fern-like leaves have 15–25mm long lobes that are oval and toothed with no stipules. Flowers are hermaphrodite and form an umbel-shaped inflorescence having eight to sixteen branches with heads of 20–60mm across. Individual flowers, 3–5mm, have five white petals, 1–2.5mm, only slightly notched. Flowers April to June.

▶ HOGWEED
Heracleum sphondylium
Family Umbelliferae

Flowering period: June to August.
Distribution: Commonplace in unimproved grassland and roadsides everywhere.
Sometimes called cow parsnip, this robust (up to

3 metres) component of tall grass communities was once gathered as pig feed, hence the name. It is a native biennial/perennial that may be bristly or not hairy at all. The hollow stems are ridged and carry divided leaves, 150–600mm long, from the base or distributed up the stem. Paired leaflets are 45–150mm, toothed and divided into irregular spear-shaped or triangular lobes. The lowermost leaves are long-stalked and sheathing stem.

Flowers are hermaphrodite and numerous in a large (50–150mm diameter) flat-topped umbel with up to twenty-five branches at stem tip. Flowers are white or pinkish, 5–10mm, with five petals (2–7mm long), deeply notched and unequal on the outer flowers. There are five small sepals, five stamens and two stigmas on short styles.
Similar species: GIANT HOGWEED (*H. mantegazzianum*) is unmistakable due to its colossal size, growing as it does up to 5 metres tall with flowering umbels a half metre across. The stems are often blotched purple. It is a less common sight on waste ground and waysides between June and July.

▶ BURNET SAXIFRAGE
Pimpinella saxifraga
Family Umbelliferae

Flowering period: May to September.
Distribution: Frequent in disused limestone quarries, pastures and rough grasslands on calcareous soils. Rare or absent from arable and rural areas, and those with acidic soils.

Growing to height of 100cm, this downy upright native perennial has slightly ridged stems carrying basal leaves (greyish beneath) with six to fourteen mostly paired leaflets, each 10–25mm. The latter are pointed oval and toothed resembling those of salad burnet. Stem leaves are infrequent or scattered and divided into thin leaflets.

Sometimes referred to as meadow pimpernel, this slender plant has white flowers, 2–3mm, having no bracts and carried in flat-topped umbels of 20–50mm wide. The stalk is longer than an individual flower; there are five minuscule sepals, five curved petals (0.5–1.5mm long), five stamens and two stigmas.
Similar species: GREATER BURNET SAXIFRAGE (*P. major*) is a much taller, hairless plant with larger leaves, all of them pinnate, and flowers that are often pink. Habitat comprises rough grassland,

TOP: BURNET SAXIFRAGE. BELOW LEFT: SWEET CICELY. RIGHT: HOGWEED.

riversides and lowland road hedgebanks. Similar flowering time.

◗ WILD PRIVET
Ligustrum vulgare
Family Oleaceae

Flowering period: May to June.
Distribution: Not so common. Scattered through lowland calcareous country of the Wolds and NYM. Less frequent in the Dales than to the east.

A native semi-evergreen of open woodland and hedgerows. Growing to heights of 5 metres this spindly shrub bears curving, shiny green leathery leaves. The latter are untoothed lanceolate and round-tipped growing in opposite pairs, sometimes turning slightly bronze. Flowers are pungent and white or creamy, carried in short pyramidal spikes. These are followed by round green, later shiny black fruits that are poisonous.
Similar species: GARDEN PRIVET (*L. ovalifolium*) often occurs as an escape where it has colonized former gardens or hedgerows and copses. It has much broader leaves.

◗ WHITE CLOVER
Trifolium repens
Family Leguminosae

Flowering period: May to November.
Distribution: Common among grasslands throughout.

This creeping perennial has a large altitude range. Growing to 50cm the more or less hairless stems bear long-stalked alternate trifoliate leaves with heart-shaped or oval leaflets, 10–30mm in length, sometimes bearing whitish markings. The globular heads are 15–30mm in diameter and formed from many hermaphrodite flowers, some 8–10mm long.

Flowers may be pink or purplish, but are more usually white turning brown. Five sepals are joined to form a narrow, almost bell-shaped calyx with narrow pointed teeth half the length of the tube. The angle between the sepal teeth is acute. There are ten stamens and one stigma.
Similar species: ALSIKE CLOVER (*T. hybridum*) is widespread in lowland habitats. It is a more erect plant with unmarked leaves and pink flowers in shorter-stalked heads with blunt angles between the sepal teeth. Flowers June to September.

◗ PURGING FLAX
Linum catharticum
Family Linaceae

Flowering period: May to September.
Distribution: Very common in the NYM and Dales, less frequent elsewhere.

This is a diminutive native perennial of limestone grasslands and upland heath, often unnoticed. Its delicacy is fitting for its alternative name of fairy flax. Growing to 25cm, the hairless stems are upright, often blackish, bearing alternating paired (often pointing upwards) leaves 5–12mm long that are spear-shaped or oblong.

The tiny white flowers are hermaphrodite and 5–7mm, several of them born on wire-like stalks in a widely branched head. The bracts are slender, the lowermost leaf-like. There are five sepals, 2–3mm, and five petals, 4–6mm, oval with rounded edge. The five stamens are joined at base, the stigma club-shaped. The plant is a relative of the cultivated flax used in the manufacture of linen.
Similar species: FLAX (*L. usitatissium*) is an escaped crop, occasionally found on waste ground. Rare in the Dales and scattered in NYM, the magnesian limestone and VoY.

◗ WHITE BRYONY
Bryonia cretica
Family Cistaceae

Flowering period: May to September.
Distribution: Near its northern limit for Britain. Scattered and infrequent on the magnesian limestone belt and in the VoY. Very rare anywhere else including the Dales and NYM.

A native and attractive perennial climber reaching heights of 4 metres, found in hedgerows. The stiffly hairy stems are angled and use unbranched tendrils at base of leaf axils as an aid to twining. Leaves (50–100mm) have five radiating lobes with wavy margins. Stipules are absent and the leaf stalk shorter than the blade.

Male and female flowers (12–18mm diameter) occur on different plants. They have five pale greenish-streaked white petals. These are hairy, oblong and joined at the base. There are five triangular sepals also joined at the base, five stamens and three two-lobed stigmas. Bracts are absent. The fruit are red and very poisonous.
Similar species: None.

TOP: WILD PRIVET. MIDDLE LEFT: PURGING FLAX. RIGHT: WHITE CLOVER. BELOW: WHITE BRYONY.

❯ ORANGE HAWKWEED

Hieracium aurantiacum agg.
Family Compositae

Flowering period: June to August
Distribution: Scattered throughout the county, but not common.

Introduced from central Europe as a garden plant, but now naturalized on roadsides, hedgebanks, waste ground and railtrack ballast. Also known as fox and cubs, this medium (to 30cm) perennial herb is covered in blackish hairs. The mainly unbranching stem rises from a basal rosette of pale green, untoothed lanceolate or oval leaves. Daisy-like flowers are 15–30mm diameter and are composed of orange or orange-red ray florets only and grow in a tight cluster of up to ten in number.
Similar species: None.

❯ RIBWORT PLANTAIN

Plantago lanceolata
Family Plantaginaceae

Flowering period: April to August.
Distribution: Abundant in all grasslands except high moorlands on soils with a pH value below 7.

Also called ribgrass, or soldiers, this low, hairless or downy native has long-stalked leaves that are 100–300mm long and form a rosette; lanceolate and slightly toothed with three to five prominent longitudinal ribs. The leaf stem is usually half the length of the blade. From this basal leaf cluster the grooved stems rise to 50cm. The hermaphrodite flowers form a brownish spike 10–15mm long. Bracts are oval and long-pointed. There are four partly joined sepals, four petals, four protruding stamens and one slender stigma. The anthers are pale yellow or white. A handful of leaves boiled for a few minutes with a quarter pint of milk, dabbed on the skin when cool is said to ease sunburn.
Similar species: The GREATER PLANTAIN (*P. major*) or rat's tail, is an equally common native perennial growing to a height of 15cm from a rosette of broad oval or elliptical leaves with longitudinal ribs. It has hairless or downy unfurrowed stems carrying pale greenish-yellow or pale brown flowers on green spikes. Anthers are pale purple becoming yellowish-brown. Flowers June to October. Common on roadsides and waste ground.

❯ BULRUSH

Typha latifolia
Family Typhaceae

Flowering period: July to August.
Distribution: Common on magnesian limestone belt, rare in the NYM; infrequent elsewhere.

Also known as cat's tail and reedmace. A creeping natural aquatic perennial of lowland marshes, pond and lake margins, canals and slow-moving fresh water. It is a stout (up to 2 metres tall) and aggressive, patch-forming plant. Leaves are lance-shaped, flat and greyish, being 10–20mm broad.

The hermaphrodite flowers (10–15cm long) form a tightly-packed contiguous spike, the lowermost (female) being chocolate brown and velvety looking like a hotdog, on top of which the male flower is straw-coloured and hairy-looking.
Similar species: LESSER BULRUSH (*T. angustifolia*) is more slender, main distinguishing feature the gap between male and female flowers.

❯ LORDS AND LADIES

Arum maculatum
Family Aracea

Flowering period: April to May.
Distribution: Common throughout the region. Favours calcareous soils in shady and damp places.

This native perennial species of the arum lilies is a poisonous plant also referred to as cuckoo pint, parson-in-the-pulpit and by other colloquial names reflecting the similarity of the flowering parts to the male and female human genitalia. It has glossy leaves, 70–200mm long, that are arrow-shaped and sometimes dark spotted, all growing from the base. Flowers are complex and appear on a central, hairless spike up to 50cm tall.

The unusual plant comprises an outer pale green sheath-like bract (spathe), surrounding a central purple, dark red or brown spike (spadix). The tiny male and female flower parts are located at the base of the spadix. This emits an aroma attractive to small insects, which are funnelled into the base of the plant by the spathe where they are trapped until they have pollinated the plant.
Similar species: BOG ARUM (*Calla palustris*) is a much smaller plant with unspotted heart-shaped glossy leaves, a shorter green spadix and a white spathe. Flowers from June to August. Aquatic, but sometimes found in damp places by still water.

TOP: ORANGE HAWKWEED. MIDDLE LEFT: BULRUSH. RIGHT: LORDS AND LADIES. BELOW: RIBWORT PLANTAIN.

4

The orchids

Orchids are certainly special. In appearance they can either be spectacularly beautiful, like the lady's slipper, or downright drab in the case of the bird's nest orchid. They may be over 60cm tall or as little as 3cm. There are over fifty species endemic to Britain, over twenty of which are found in Yorkshire, some commonplace, others very rare indeed.

Plants of the family Orchidicaea differ somewhat from other vascular plants in being perennials growing either from tubers, fleshy rooting stock (rhizomes), or pseudobulbs which in unfavourable seasons provide the food source. An annual aerial, and unbranched, stem carries the flowers in an upright spike. Depending on the species this may consist of anything from one to one hundred flowers. In the majority of helleborines the flowers are born in a lax, one-sided spike, the individual blooms slightly drooping. With few exceptions (Epipactis) the plants are hairless.

Saprophytic orchids, such as coral root (*Corallorhiza trifida*) and bird's nest (*Neottia nidus-avis*) live in the darkest parts of forests, usually beech, and are virtually lacking green pigment (chlorophyll). They are not dependent on sunlight and obtain almost all nutrients from the deep decaying humus of the forest floor. Leaves are reduced to scale-like appendages sheathing the base of the stem. All other orchids have fleshy looking leaves that are unstalked, non-toothed and undivided but keeled with parallel veins.

SYMBIOTIC LIFE-CYCLE

In order to survive, orchids live in symbiosis with specific mycorrhiza fungi. This is a fine fungus mycelium present among the roots of other plants. These fungi, of which several distinct species have been identified, are essential for germination of orchids; however after the fungus attacks the host, it is then consumed by the cells of the orchid. This process follows a cycle, the fungus and the orchid in turn seasonally dominating the other: fungal dominance takes place during the winter, but in the summer the role is reversed. As the plant matures fungal dependence varies, some orchids becoming totally independent, while others are generally dependant on the fungus for their entire life.

STRUCTURE

In orchid flowers it is difficult to separate the coloured petals (corolla) and green sepals (calyx); therefore these are collectively referred to under the term perianth. In most orchids the three sepals (outer perianth components), two lateral and one dorsal, form an approximate star-shape. These play a more prominent role in the appearance of the orchid than is the case with most other flowering plants. Unlike most of the latter, the sepals in orchids can be very colourful.

The petals (inner perianth) consist of two lateral members and one ventral. The two lateral, uppermost petals and the dorsal sepal combine to form a more or less loose hood, while the ventral lobe forms the labellum (lip) and in effect provides a landing stage for insects. The lip may be delicately streaked and spotted, and in some cases large, unusual or showy as in the lizard orchid and lady's slipper. At the rear of the lip the latter forms a hollow spur in some species and contains the nectar to attract pollinating insects.

REPRODUCTION

Reproduction of orchids varies. Only in those rhizomatous species is vegetative increase possible, that is by branching of the rhizome itself. In tuberous orchids reproduction is by seeds. Orchids employ some startlingly ingenious methods of pollination. With bee and fly orchids, for example, ingenious insect mimicry is used to attract a specific vector, which then attempts to copulate with the flower. This sexual deception is aided by the plant releasing scents resembling those of the female insect.

The lady's slipper has for many decades been the subject of the Endangered Species Recovery Programme, an initiative run jointly between English Nature (now Natural England) and Kew Gardens. The unique relationship between orchids and fungus is one of the fundamental difficulties facing those attempting to propagate new plants. Though the one colony of lady's slipper continues to thrive, attempts to reintroduce it into the old habitats elsewhere, after over twenty years, are only now beginning to enjoy limited success.

HABITAT

Orchids are found in most habitats. They are very sensitive to climatic conditions, light availability, moisture and soil types. Plants may lay dormant for years, only flowering when the conditions suit. Again, even if a plant sends up new stems, they may not always bear flowers. Some species, notably lady's slipper, take several years – as many as fifteen – in order to reach sufficient maturity to flower for the first time.

IDENTIFICATION

Identification is not always easy. Some, such as the bee, butterfly and fragrant orchids, and the helleborines, are not too difficult, but plants of the Dactylorhiza group have many subspecies and hybrids, identification of which can prove a real test for the enthusiast. But therein lies part of the enjoyment of flower hunting. I would recommend that readers join one of the flower societies (see the address list and bibliography).

❭ FLY ORCHID
Ophrys insectifera
Family Orchidaceae

Flowering period: May to June.
Distribution: Very rare. Formerly much more widespread; the rapid decline brought about by loss of habitat. This native tuber is more common in the NYM than the Dales, where it is known from only one location in ancient woodland.

This is a most unusual plant, and an astounding example of insect mimicry. The plant grows to heights of 15–60cm with a slender stem normally having three narrow lower leaves (up to 10cm long) that are dark green and shiny. The bracts are leaf-like and erect. The inflorescence is extremely lax and can have from two to ten small flowers.

The sepals are yellow-green, pointed and slightly inclined forward. The inner perianth segments closely resemble a fly, the lateral segments being thread like to mimic insect antennae. The labellum is 8–13mm long and is brown with three lobes, the lateral ones resembling small wings, the lowermost being longer, notched and representing the body of the fly. It has a white or blue band at its base, though this may be pale or absent altogether.
Similar species: None.

❭ BEE ORCHID
Ophrys apifera
Family Orchidaceae

Flowering period: June to July.
Distribution: Fairly widespread in the Dales, Wolds and the magnesian limestones, less so in NYM. Also found east of Leeds on old coal mine sites. A plant reputed to be spreading its range, though nowhere can it be regarded as prolific.

This unusual native perennial has a lower perianth member resembling a female bumble bee to encourage the male insect to visit and pollinate the flower. Growing to a height of up to 45cm the pale green single stem has elliptical leaves that are pointed and clasping the stem. By the time the flowers appear the leaves have generally withered.

Flowers (usually three) have pink sepals, green petals and a lip that is velvety in texture and reddish-brown, rounded at the tip and patterned to resemble a bee. This is one of the few native orchids that are quick to colonize recently disturbed calcareous ground, and can be found on long-disused industrial sites, abandoned quarries and grass verges; even central reservations on busy roads.
Similar species: None.

❭ COMMON TWAYBLADE
Listera ovata
Family Orchidaceae

Flowering period: May to July.
Distribution: Commonplace on alkaline soils throughout in unimproved grasslands, shady woods, hedgerows and limestone pavement grikes.

A robust and often dominant plant of its habitat, this native perennial is one of the most abundant orchid flowers. It grows to heights of up 60cm, the most obvious feature being the twin (very rarely three), pointed oval leaves that lend the name to the species. These are broad, 50–200mm long, with three to five prominent longitudinal veins.

The single upright stem bears a raceme of some 70–250mm in length comprising many (up to eighty or more) individual 12–20mm long, greenish-yellow flowers. Bracts are present but are shorter than the flowers. The dorsal and lateral sepals, plus lateral petals form a hood, while the labellum, 10–15mm in length, is without spur and is deeply forked and often bent backwards towards the stem, the overall affect rather like a tiny man with a big head.
Similar species: LESSER TWAYBLADE (*L. cordata*) is scarce. It is found in the NYM, less so in the Dales and on Rombalds Moor. It is a less conspicuous plant, growing to only 10cm but often no bigger than 5cm. There is a single pair of heart-shaped leaves at the base of the stem from which the slender stem carries tiny reddish green flowers. The labellum is vaguely three-lobed, the central lobe forked. Petals and sepals are half hooded. Favoured habitat is moorland and bogs, often partially hidden beneath bracken or heather. Flowers June to August.

TOP: BEE ORCHID. BELOW LEFT AND INSET: FLY ORCHID. BELOW RIGHT AND INSET: COMMON TWAYBLADE.

⟩ DARK RED HELLEBORINE

Epipactis atrorubens
Family Orchidaceae

Flowering period: June to July.
Distribution: Rare. Found in the YDNP area
where it is known from a few rocky limestone
pastures and pavements, also from two or three
sites near Kippax, east of Leeds.

This native rhizome is a handsome plant preferring
sheltered habitats such as grikes or fissures in scars
and rocky places. The plant has numerous long
and thin roots ideally suited to probing for moisture
deep into rocky fissures. The stem, 3–4mm
diameter, may be as much as 60cm tall, downy and
red-tinged, carrying five to seven dark green leaves
that are broad and arranged alternately in two
rows. The lowermost are oval and the upper leaves
elongated and rough to the touch.

Both stem and flowers are covered in a dense
coating of fine hairs, which close up impart a
velvety appearance to the plant. Flowers (up to
twenty in a one-sided raceme, but usually fewer
than ten) are slightly drooping, fragrant (vanilla
scented) and a wonderful deep wine red or
maroon in colour. Bracts are equal to, or longer
than the flowers. The dorsal sepal and lateral
petals are pointed oval and overlap forming almost
a cup enclosing the labellum. The latter has no
spur and is 5–6.5mm long.
Similar species: None.

⟩ MARSH HELLEBORINE

Epipactis palustris
Family Orchidaceae

Flowering period: July to August.
Distribution: Very rare. This most beautiful of
plants is declining nationally. Known from a
handful of locations in the Dales, even fewer in the
NYM. Most Dales specimens are known from
Wharfedale, though a recent discovery near the
western fringe of the YDNP suggests the species is
extending its range.

A component of flushed areas and calcareous
wetlands, it grows to 60cm with two to four
sheathing scale leaves and four to eight lanceolate
stem leaves, 7–20cm long and 1.5–4cm wide.
These are keeled, folded and slightly clasping the
stem. Each has three prominent longitudinal veins.
The base of the stem and the leaves often have

violet sheaths. The flower spike (6–20cm long) is
lax and one-sided carrying between seven and
twenty flowers. This is one of those blooms that to
be fully appreciated one must be on all fours with
a magnifier.

The perianth segments are extremely
colourful, the outer ones (sepals) being pointed
and a purple or purplish-brown, and the upper
inner perianth segment white, tinged with pink or
crimson near the base. The large labellum (up to
13mm long) is broad, white and divided into two
parts: the upper (hypochile) and the lower
(epichile), both joined by a hinge. The cup-
shaped hypochile has prominent red veins and two
lateral 'ears', while the lower half of the labellum,
the epichile, has a frilly outer edge and is white
with a yellow throat.
Similar species: BROAD-LEAVED HELLEBORINE
(*E. helleborine*) is more common (less so in the
NYM) but scarce still. It grows to 90cm and
prefers lightly shaded deciduous woodland. In the
NYM it has established itself in a few shady places
along disused coastal rail track. Flowers are
variable and may be greenish-yellow to purplish-
red, grouped in a one-sided spike with as many as
100 in number.

⟩ EARLY PURPLE ORCHID

Orchis Mascula
Family Orchidaceae

Flowering period: April to June.
Distribution: Common throughout on most soils,
most usually found in light woods, scrub and
grassy places.

The upright stems are from 15–60cm tall and rise
from a rosette comprising up to eight spear-shaped
or oblong leaves. These are blotched with dark
purple, the upper ones being distinctly scale-like.
The degree of markings include leaves completely
without any. The flowers form a spike of
40–150mm in length. The inflorescence, which
may occasionally be lax, can contain as many as
fifty flowers of reddish-purple sometimes pink or
(less common) white. Those growing in woodland
tend to have the most flowers.

Blooms have rounded sepals, the uppermost
forming a hood, with two petals standing erect like
a pair of 'rabbit's ears' in appearance, the two
remaining sepals being folded way back behind
the flower. The lower perianth segment is the

TOP LEFT: EARLY PURPLE ORCHID. TOP RIGHT AND INSET: DARK RED HELLEBORINE. BELOW AND INSET: MARSH HELLEBORINE.

larger and forms a shallowly three-lobed lip with a long robust spur that curves or points upwards. The central lobe is longest and has a notched tip. The edges of all the lobes are crenellated.
Similar species: None.

▶ FRAGRANT ORCHID
Gymnadenia conopsea
Family Orchidaceae

Flowering period: June to August.
Distribution: Fairly common in the Dales, NYM, seacliff grasslands and alkaline grassy places elsewhere. Found along roadside verges, hay meadows and other unimproved grasslands, also occasionally in disused limestone quarries.

Growing up to 75cm, this plant has an inflorescence that can contain as many as two hundred individual blooms. There are three to five spotted lanceolate leaves at the base of the plant. These may be folded and slightly hooded. Higher up the stem they become more scale-like, narrow and pointed. The bracts are slightly shorter or equal to the flowers, and are green and pointed.

Flowers are normally a wonderfully purplish-pink or rich pink (occasionally white) grouped in an elongated inflorescence. Flowers have spreading sepals and hooded petals with a distinctly three-lobed lip and very long delicate spur. The central lobe is shaped like an isosceles triangle. The lengthy lateral sepals are aligned downwards and outwards either side of the broad lip. This is one of the most easily identified of all our orchids by virtue of its wonderful clove-like bouquet.
Similar species: None.

▶ FROG ORCHID
Coeloglossum viride
Family Orchidaceae

Flowering period: June into July.
Distribution: Scarce and in decline. More common in the Dales than the NYM, or even the Wolds, though it can still be found in a few scattered locations in these areas.

A plant of hilly grasslands – short, grazed turf, sometimes on hummocks or on grassy patches within limestone pavements. This secretive little perennial tuber sometimes grows up to 35cm but is often just a few centimetres and therefore goes unnoticed in the grass. The leaves, 10cm long and 5cm wide, are lanceolate and narrowing up the stem. Bracts are long and leafy, usually pointed, the lowest being much longer than the flowers, the uppermost shorter or equal in length to the flowers.

Though the inflorescence may only be formed of a couple of dozen flowers, it can have over forty. The unusual flowers are yellowish-green, tinged along the margins with red-brown; sepals and petals are hooded, short and broad. The lip is strap-shaped, 5–9mm long, with two parallel lateral lobes and one central lobe forming a small tooth. The spur is grooved and very short at 2–3mm in length.
Similar species: None.

▶ GREATER BUTTERFLY ORCHID
Platanthera chlorantha
Family Orchidaceae

Flowering period: June to July.
Distribution: Scarce. Scattered in the NYM, mostly along the southern fringes, and in the Dales. Also known from a few locations on the magnesian limestone.

This wonderful native perennial is one of the most distinctive of our orchid species. It is a delicate-looking plant favouring unimproved grassland, traditional hay meadows, open woodland and roadsides on calcareous soils. Growing to heights in the region of 40cm, the upright stems are quite slender and emerge from a pair of broad, shiny elliptical leaves. These are up to 150mm in length. Further leaves decrease in size and become lanceolate, arranged spirally up the stem.

Flowers are creamy white, tinged pale green or lemon, forming an inflorescence, 50–200mm long, containing between ten to twenty-five individual blooms. These appear loosely grouped since they stand well clear of the stem on long ovaries. The two upper sepals, together with the upper petal, represent a loose hood. The third petal, forming the labellum, is strap-like and very long, forming a convenient 'landing pad' for insects come to pollinate the flower. The two pollen-bearing organs (the pollinia), are either side of the entrance to the spur and are angled inward and forward, the two being nearest at their uppermost end.
Similar species: Rare. The LESSER BUTTERFLY ORCHID (*P. bifolia*) is known from a few scattered

TOP LEFT: FRAGRANT ORCHID. RIGHT: FROG ORCHID. BELOW: GREATER BUTTERFLY ORCHID.

localities in both the NYM area and the Dales. It is a much shorter and smaller plant though size is not a reliable indicator of ssp. The arrangement of the two pollinia is the principal aid in differentiating this plant from *P. chlorantha*. In this case they are parallel.

▶ COMMON SPOTTED ORCHID
Dactylorhiza fuchsii
Family Orchidaceae

Flowering period: June to August.
Distribution: The most abundant of the marsh-loving orchids ranging throughout the Dales and NYM, VoY and the Wolds. Also found in the magnesian limestone belt, parts of West and South Yorkshire.

Mostly found in unimproved grassland and scrub on calcareous soils up to altitudes of 500 metres. Surprisingly for Dactylorhiza, the plant has adapted to quite dry conditions, and been effective at colonizing railway embankments, road verges and forest fringes.

This medium-height perennial has a stout, upright stem to 45cm bearing as many as twenty lanceolate leaves from the base, with three to five shorter, clasping leaves higher up. Leaves are narrow, keeled and with markings varying from hardly any to an almost complete covering of purply-brown blotches.

The flowers are pale purple, pink or white, dotted and streaked with crimson or purple, formed into a long, tapering spike that has densely crowded flowers. There are three oval petal-like sepals with three unequal petals; two of them oval and inclined upwards which, together with the two upper petals, form a hood. The third petal comprises the prominently three-lobed labellum, the two side lobes being rhomboid in shape, the central tooth triangular. A useful aid to identification is the fact that the lip has prominent symmetrical double loops formed of broken lines and dots of purple or dark mauve. The spur is cylindrical and not tapering. It can be almost 7mm long.
Similar species: See HEATH SPOTTED ORCHID (*D. maculata*).

▶ HEATH SPOTTED ORCHID
Dactylorhiza maculata
Family Orchidacea

Flowering period: June to August.
Distribution: Rarely found in limestone country. Scarce in the Dales and more widespread in the NYM. One of the least common of the marsh orchids.

Generally found on heaths, moors and marshes with a more acid or neutral sub-soil. The labellum also lacks the double loop marking that is a clear feature identifying the common spotted orchid. The plant is less robust and growing to heights of 40cm, though more usually no higher than 25cm. Up to eight narrow, pointed leaves are clasping and only slightly spotted, or not at all. The inflorescence is pyramid-shaped and short, with a very pale pinkish or white coloration to the perianth segments.

The labellum is broad, 6.5–15mm, and flat with a wavy edge lacking the prominent central tooth of the *D. fuchsii*; the lateral lobes being rounded and the central lobe triangular in shape and often shorter than the lateral ones. The 4–12mm long spur is cylindrical and not as stout as in *D. fuchsii*. The markings of the lip and lateral sepals consist of delicate short lines and dots of red. The lateral sepals, 5–11mm, are inclined forward, and lateral petals 3.5–8mm long. The two upper petals and upper sepal form a loose hood.
Similar species: None.

▶ NORTHERN MARSH ORCHID
Dactylorhiza purpurella
Family Orchidaceae

Flowering period: June to July.
Distribution: Fairly commonplace throughout on unimproved grassland, beside streams and in wet flushes along the coast and cliff tops.

The northern marsh orchid is a root tuber but not as common as *Orchis mascula*. First recognized as a distinct species in 1920, it is also known by its other common name, dwarf purple orchid. Its deep wine-purple flowers make it quite a handsome plant. Growing to 25cm it sometimes has slight spotting near the apex of the leaves. The latter are generally quite broad, but the plant can also tolerate a lower pH value, and under such conditions the leaves are often narrower. Bracts are

TOP: HEATH SPOTTED ORCHID. BELOW LEFT: COMMON SPOTTED ORCHID. RIGHT: NORTHERN MARSH ORCHID.

unspotted and shorter than in *Orchis mascula*. Flowers have a broad labellum, sometimes curling upwards. It is spotted or streaked, and can be untoothed or shallowly-lobed with a thick, tapering spur. The inflorescence is a distinctive aid to positive identification, as it appears truncated as if the upper half has been cut off. It contains up to twenty flowers, the rich coloration of which is not found in other British orchids.
Similar species: There are a number of other marsh orchids that are difficult to separate. SOUTHERN MARSH ORCHID (*D. praetermissa*) is not as common as *D. purpurella*. It differs from the latter in being a more stalwart plant with an inflorescence that does not appear truncated.

▶ PYRAMID ORCHID
Anacamptis pyramidalis
Family Orchidaceae

Flowering period: June to August.
Distribution: Widespread but scarce in the Dales. More common on the magnesian limestone, the NYM and Wolds areas. Also on the cliffs at Flamborough, in the SPNNR and at SFNR in South Yorkshire and disused coal tips east of Leeds.

This is one of earliest plants to colonize old quarries, disused railway tracks and other industrial sites, also being found on roadside verges and in wet flushes in other grassy places. The stem is slender, 3–5mm diameter, with upward pointing scale-like narrow stem leaves. The inflorescence only appears pyramidal in shape when the uppermost flowers have not yet opened, after which the flowerhead becomes more globular in shape. Flowers are a pale to rich pink or pale purple, very rarely white. The labellum is broad and flat with three more or less equal, rounded lobes.
Similar species: None.

▶ LADY'S SLIPPER
Cypripedium calceolus
Family Orchidaceae

Flowering period: May to June.
Distribution: Extremely rare. Occurring naturally only in one location in North Yorkshire, Britain's sole extant colony.

The lady's slipper is the most beautiful of British orchids. First recorded from woods near Ingleton in 1640, it favours limestone mountain woods and scrub. This is a large and showy plant, growing up to 60cm tall. The single stem bears broad, pale green lanceolate leaves that are strongly ribbed, up to five of them arranged alternately, sheathing the stem.

Stems normally support only a single flower. The latter has petals and sepals of a deep maroon or claret colour, the lateral petals twisted and up to 3cm in length. The bright yellow inflated labellum is hollow with red spots on the inside surface. With a length of 2–3cm this is the most obvious feature of the plant.
Similar species: None.

LEFT: PYRAMID ORCHID. RIGHT: LADY'S SLIPPER.

Glossary

acid soils   soils formed on substrates such as millstone grit and sandstone, or overlaid with a depth of peat deposits.

aggregate   (agg.) a plant group consisting of many related species or subspecies.

alien   plant introduced and become naturalized, not native.

alluvial   refers to soil or silt deposited by flowing water.

alternate   of leaves that are alternately arranged up the stem as opposed to opposite, spirally or in whorls.

annual   a plant living its entire life cycle within one season.

anther   the tip of the stamen producing male pollen.

axil   angle between a stem and leaf.

basal   appertaining to the base of a plant.

base   water or soil having a pH value greater than 7, in other words alkaline.

berry   the fleshy fruit of some plants.

biennial   a plant with life cycle spanning two seasons, the first year usually producing leaves followed by flowers in the second season.

bog   habitat of wet acid peat, often dominated by sphagnum moss.

boulder clay   till or glacial clay deposit consisting of pebbles and rocks ranging to boulder size.

bract   leaf-like organs immediately beneath the flower, at the junction of the flower stalk and the stem.

bulb   sub-soil food storage organ composed of concentric layers of fleshy leaves.

bulbil   small bulb-like growth in the leaf axils.

calcareous soil   base-rich soil overlaying limestone or chalk strata.

calcicole   a plant favouring base-rich soil.

calcifuge   plants preferring neutral to acid soil.

calyx   term used to describe the outer ring of flower organs, the sepals, when joined together.

carpel   the female organ in a flower, enclosing one or more ovules.

carr   waterlogged woodland.

catkin   suspended flower tassel formed of rather inconspicuous individual flowers.

chlorophyll   green pigment in plants that convert sun's energy in a process known as photosynthesis.

clasping   refers to the way some leaves partially or wholly embrace the stem.

clint   see limestone pavement.

cluster   a loose group of flowers.

column   top of the stem bearing the orchid flower.

composite   member of the Compositae (daisy family).

corm   bulb-like sub-soil food storage organ consisting of a swelling of the stem base.

corolla   the inner ring of organs of a flower, the petals, when joined together.

corona   bell, cup or tube-shaped extension from the centre of a flower.

crest   name given to the branching tip of the petal-like stigma in flowers of the iris family.

crucifer   a member of the Cruciferae or cabbage family.

deciduous   refers to woody plants that lose their leaves in autumn.

deflexed   bent downwards.

dioecious   with male and female organs on separate plants.

disk florets   the many tiny central flowers of a composite flower head, forming a disk as in a daisy.

endemic   native to an area, region or country.

epicalyx   ring formed by sepal-like organs immediately beneath the true sepals.

epichile   the lower half of the labellum in some orchids, notably helleborines.

ericaceous   refers to plants of the heather family.

evergreen   woody plants that retain their leaves the whole year.

falls   the outer petals of flowers of the iris family.

family   grouping of living forms greater than genus.

female flower   containing styles, but not stamens.

fen   a habitat formed on lime-rich peat, as opposed to acid bog.

filament   the stalk of a stamen.

florets   the tiny flowers comprising a compound or composite flowerhead; see disk floret and ray floret.

flower   reproductive part of a vascular plant.

flowerhead   flowers found in tightly packed formal heads (aggregated), as in species of the daisy family for instance.

flushed grassland   grassland that is frequently flushed by calcium-rich water from springs or overflow from streams and caves, where seeping water fans out over a wide area.

foetid   with a strong, unpleasant smell.

fruit   the seeds of a plant and the tissue structure enclosing them; it may be either fleshy as in a berry, or dry like a nut.

genus   taxonomic grouping (below family) of closely related forms that is further subdivided into species.

glabrous   having a smooth, hairless surface.

glaucous   having a waxy bloom lending a grey or bluish coloration.

grikes   fissures that divide the flat limestone pavements (clints) in karst landscapes.

gritstone   acid-based rock strata.

habitat   the collective climatic, topographic and geographical features forming a specific bios.

head   individual flowers grouped in a compact terminal group (see umbel)

heath   habitat on acid soil, dominated usually by heather and related plants.

herb	a vascular plant without a woody stem.
hermaphrodite	plant having both male and female reproductive organs.
hip	false fruit, brightly-coloured and peculiar to the Rosaceae (rose) family.
hoary	refers to plants covered in short hairs and greyish in appearance.
humus	layers of decaying vegetable matter, dead leaves etc, accumulating on the forest floor.
hybrid	a cross between two distinct plant species.
hypochile	upper part of the labellum in some orchids, notably the helleborines.
improved grassland	grassland or arable farmland that has been ploughed, perhaps re-seeded and chemically treated to increase yield.
inflorescence	the flowering branch or branches, including the bracts, positioned above the uppermost leaves on a stem.
ing	a water meadow.
insectivorous	describes a plant obtaining some or all of its nutrients by digesting insects.
introduced	refers to a plant that is not native.
karst	derived from the Slovenian kras, now used to describe any landscape displaying typical limestone features, such as dry valleys, sinkholes, clints and grikes.
keel	the single central rib of a leaf, as is normal in those of orchids; also applies to the lower petal of flowers in the pea family.
labiate	refers to plants belonging to the mint or Labiatae family.
lanceolate	having narrow, spear-like leaves, more or less elliptical.
lax	describes a flowerhead that is loose, or well-spaced, rather than a dense spike.
legume	of the pea family.
lime-rich soil	having a pH higher than the value 7.
limestone pavement	a post-glacial landform in which glaciers have scoured limestone strata leaving flat pavement-like rock outcrops (clints) divided by fissures known as grikes.
linear	parallel-sided.
lip	lowermost petal of a labiate flower, or of most orchid flowers; two-lipped flowers have both upper and lower lips, the uppermost usually being a hood.
lobed	describes leaves that are deeply toothed but not pinnate, as in having separate leaflets; also appertains to the petal divisions of flowers as in ventral perianth, or lip, of an orchid.
magnesian	limestone strata rich in the metallic element magnesium (Mg).
male flower	containing the male only (stamens) reproductive organs and not styles.
marsh	wetland habitat without peat.
microspecies	those produced by reproductive processes resulting in a great many biologically distinct units.
midrib	the medial or central vein in a leaf.
montane	describes a plant native to or inhabiting mountainous country.

moor	an upland area covered with heather and related species.
morphology	the scientific study of the form and appearance of a living species.
mycorrhiza	a root fungus on which some plants are dependent for growth.
native	naturally occurring.
naturalized	species that has become established outside of its area of normal distribution.
nectar	sugary excretion produced by some flowers to attract insects.
nectary	the nectar-producing organ in a flower.
node	point on a stem from which a leaf originates.
officinalis	when used in a botanical name, indicates a plant and herbs once used for medicinal purposes.
opposite	describes leaves arranged opposite each other on the stem, not spirally, alternate or whorls.
ovary	the female organ containing the ovules.
palate	projecting area adjacent to the mouth of a flower.
palmate	refers to the splayed finger arrangement of a leaf or leaflets.
palmately lobed	divided like the fingers of a hand.
pappus	the thistle-down – tufts of hairs forming the 'parachutes' of dandelion and thistle fruits.
parasite	plant obtaining its nourishment from another plant; see saprophite.
peat	acidic soil derived from the undecayed accumulations of plant debris.
pedicel	a stalk bearing only one flower.
perennial	a plant that lives for several years; plants of this type are often more robust, sometimes woody even.
perianth	the collective term for sepals and petals where these are difficult to distinguish from one another, as in orchids.
petal	prominent organ – the inner perianth segment, often coloured, located above the sepals and encompassing the sexual organs.
pH value	a measure of the soil's level of acidity; a value below 7 indicates acidity and one above, alkalinity.
pinnate	refers to the arrangement of leaflets forming a leaf, sometimes ladder-like in appearance, for example two or more pairs of parallel leaflets, with or without a terminal leaflet.
pinnately lobed	describes a leaf that is divided in a pinnate fashion without total separation into leaflets.
pod	a long and cylindrical fruit containing the seeds, vis-à-vis in the case of legumes.
pollen	tiny particles produced by the anther; see pollination.
pollination	the process, by natural or otherwise means, of transferring pollen from the anther in the male organ of a flower to the female stigma.
pollinia	aggregated pollen masses found in orchids.
prickle	a sharply pointed, sometimes hooked, projection from the surface of a stem or leaf, as in teasel or burdock plant.
prostrate	lying along the ground.

pungent	strongly aromatic.
raceme	unbranched inflorescence, often a drooping spike, consisting of many visibly stalked flowers.
ray	stalk radiating from an umbel.
ray floret	the outer component of a composite flower.
receptacle	the part of the stem from which the floral organs originate.
reflexed	turned back.
rhizome	horizontal underground stem by which some orchids reproduce by sending out new aerial stems.
rosette	a whorl, or flattened arrangement of leaves at the base of the stem.
ruderal	appertaining to a plant growing on waste ground or among rubbish.
runner	above-ground stem that extends horizontally, sometimes rooting at the nodes.
samara	a winged fruit, as in maple trees.
saprophite	plant having little or no chlorophyll (green pigment) which gains all or most of its nutrients from decomposing plant debris of the forest floor.
scales	small appendages, rather like reduced leaves, that sheath a stem; sometimes papery in appearance.
scrub	unimproved land colonized by a mix of woody shrubs and tall grassland plant species; can be considered an intermediate phase between grassland reverting to wood.
sepal	the leaf-like organs immediately beneath the petals, a component of the outer whorl of a perianth in the majority of flowers; usually green and may be insignificant, or larger than or replacing the petals.
sheath	the lowest part of a leaf clasping the stem.
shrub	a frequently branching woody plant, smaller than a tree.
spadix	the inflorescence of the arum lily.
spathe	bract-like organ, or sheath, surrounding the spadix.
species	the term adopted for the basic units of classification of a living organism; usually abbreviated sp.
spike	upright stem (inflorescence) bearing unstalked flowers arranged axially.
spine	a stiff, sharp-tipped appendage, sometimes a modified shoot.
spiral	describes leaves arranged spirally around a stem, rather than alternate, opposite or in whorls.
spreading	appertaining to stems extending at a wide-angle outwards from the central axis of the plant; also to sepals or petals where these are not joined to form a calyx or corolla.
spur	hollow cylindrical extension to the lower petal, or lip, of orchids and some other flowers.

stamen	the male reproductive organ of a flower, comprised of a filament and a pollen sac (anther); distinguished from the styles by the often coloured anthers, and that it lies outside the flower centre, normally in a ring.
standard	name given to the erect, often twisted, inner petals of flowers belong the iris family.
stigma	the surface at the tip of the style that receives the pollen.
stipule	tiny scale-like or leaf-like organ located in the angle at the base of a leaf stalk.
style	column of filaments extending from the female sexual organ (ovary) to the stigma; distinguished from stamens by lying at the centre of the flower.
subspecies	the division of the classification of organisms immediately below species; usually abbreviated to ssp.
sugar limestone	limestone that has undergone metamorphosis due to volcanic intrusions, thus altering its structure.
symbiosis	process by which two living organisms depend upon each other for their continued survival.
tendril	extension of a leaf or stem formed of twisted filaments, used as an aid to the climbing plant.
tepal	a member of the perianth that cannot clearly be identified as either calyx and corolla.
thorn	a sharp-pointed adaptation of stems to protect against grazing beasts; may be either straight or curved.
throat	opening to a tubular flower.
toothed	appertains to serrated leaf or petal margins.
tree	woody plant taller than a shrub.
trefoil, trifoliate	having three leaflets.
tube	the joined parts of a corolla or calyx.
tuber	swollen underground root or stem.
umbel	flat-toped flowerhead formed by all the flowers arranged together.
umbellifer	a member of the Umbelliferae, or carrot family.
undershrub	a prostrate, sometimes creeping woody perennial.
variety	refers to a distinct form of a plant lower than subspecies.
vein	conducting tissue, or strengthening rib, in a leaf or petal.
waste ground	that which is disturbed but uncultivated.
whorl	the circular arrangement of leaves or petals where each has originated from a single central point.
winged	refers to a stem or stalk having a flange running down the length; also the lateral petals in flowers of the pea family.

Useful addresses

Botanical Society of the British Isles
c/o British Museum (Natural History),
Cromwell Road, London SW7 5BD
www.bsbi.org.uk

Natural England (Formerly English Nature)
Government Buildings, Otley Road,
Leeds LS16 5QT
www.naturalengland.org.uk

Wild Flower Society
c/o Mike Hooper, 24 Muirfield Drive,
Astley, Manchester M29 7QJ
www.thewildflowersociety.com

Yorkshire Naturalists' Union
3 Brookmead Close, Sutton Poyntz,
Weymouth DT3 6RS
www.ynu.org.uk

Yorkshire Wildlife Trust
1 St. Georges Place, York YO24 1GN
www.yorkshire-wildlife-trust.org.uk

Further reading

Buttler, K.P., *Field Guide to Orchids of Britain and Europe* (The Crowood Press, 1986, Rev. ed., 1991)
Dony, J.G., Rob, C.M. and Perring, F.H., *English Names of Wild Flowers* (Botanical Society of the British Isles, 1974)
Lubbock, Sir J., *British Wild Flowers Considered in Relation to Insect* (Macmillan, 1890)
Mitchell, A., *A Field Guide to the Trees of Britain and Northern Europe* (Collins, 1974)

Preston, C.D, *Aquatic Plants in Britain and Ireland* (Harley Books, 1997)
Preston, C.D, Pearman, D.A and Dines, T.D. (eds.), *New Atlas of British Flora* (Oxford University Press, 2002)
Wilmore, G.T.D., *Alien Plants of Yorkshire* (Yorkshire Naturalists' Union, 2000)

Index of common names

Index of Latin names